THE WHITE HOUSE

AN HISTORIC GUIDE

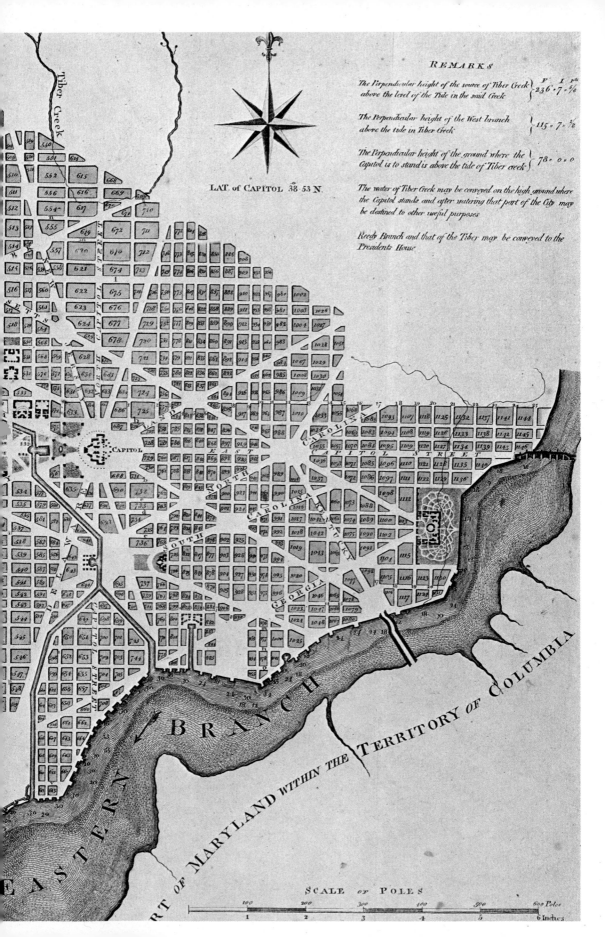

The Perpendicular height of the source of Tiber Creek
above the level of the Tide in the said Creek
} 236 . 7 . 4/8

The Perpendicular height of the West branch
above the tide in Tiber Creek
} 115 . 7 . 5/8

The Perpendicular height of the ground where the
Capitol is to stand is above the tide of Tiber creek
} 78 . 0 . 0

The water of Tiber Creek may be conveyed on the high ground where
the Capitol stands and after watering that part of the City may
be destined to other useful purposes

Reedy Branch and that of the Tiber may be conveyed to the
Presidents House

LAT. of CAPITOL 38.53 N.

Tiber Creek

CAPITOL

EAST CAPITOL STREET

NORTH CAROLINA

SOUTH CAROLINA

GEORGIA

KENTUCKY

EASTERN BRANCH

PART OF MARYLAND WITHIN THE TERRITORY OF COLUMBIA

SCALE OF POLES

100   200   300   400   500   600 Poles

1   2   3   4   5   6 Inches

The Entrance Hall seen from the North Portico, with emblems of office at the door of the Blue Room:

THE WHITE HOUSE
AN HISTORIC GUIDE

WHITE HOUSE
HISTORICAL
ASSOCIATION
*with the
cooperation
of the
National
Geographic
Society
Washington, D. C.*

the President's seal, the President's flag, and the flag of the United States.

THE WHITE HOUSE: AN HISTORIC GUIDE

TEXT CONSULTANTS: *Margaret B. Klapthor*, CURATOR EMERITUS, DIVISION OF POLITICAL HISTORY, NATIONAL MUSEUM OF AMERICAN HISTORY, SMITHSONIAN INSTITUTION; *Dr. Richard L. Watson, Jr.*, PROFESSOR OF HISTORY, DUKE UNIVERSITY

PRODUCED BY THE NATIONAL GEOGRAPHIC SOCIETY AS A PUBLIC SERVICE
Gilbert M. Grosvenor, PRESIDENT AND CHAIRMAN OF THE BOARD
Melvin M. Payne, Thomas W. McKnew, CHAIRMEN EMERITUS
Owen R. Anderson, EXECUTIVE VICE PRESIDENT
Robert L. Breeden, SENIOR VICE PRESIDENT, PUBLICATIONS AND EDUCATIONAL MEDIA
PREPARED BY THE SPECIAL PUBLICATIONS DIVISION
Donald J. Crump, DIRECTOR
Philip B. Silcott, ASSOCIATE DIRECTOR
Bonnie S. Lawrence, ASSISTANT DIRECTOR
Jody Bolt, ART DIRECTOR
Geraldine Linder, ILLUSTRATIONS RESEARCH
Steve Adams, Joseph H. Bailey, James P. Blair, Victor R. Boswell, Jr., David R. Bridge, Nelson Brown, A. Robert Cole, John E. Fletcher, Otis Imboden, Larry Kinney, Erik Kvalsvik, Philip R. Leonhardi, Bates W. Littlehales, George F. Mobley, Robert S. Oakes, Claude E. Petrone, Tom M. Pope, Martin Rogers, Cynthia B. Scudder, PHOTOGRAPHY
STAFF FOR SIXTEENTH EDITION: *Jane H. Buxton*, EDITOR; *Elizabeth W. Fisher*, RESEARCHER; *Viviane Silverman*, DESIGNER; *Hildegard B. Groves*, ARTIST; *Teresa P. Barry*, INDEXER; *Sharon K. Berry, Mary Elizabeth Ellison, Sandra F. Lotterman, Eliza C. Morton*, STAFF ASSISTANTS
ENGRAVING, PRINTING, AND PRODUCT MANUFACTURE: *Robert W. Messer*, MANAGER; *George V. White*, SENIOR ASSISTANT MANAGER; *Vincent P. Ryan*, ASSISTANT MANAGER; *David V. Showers*, PRODUCTION MANAGER; *Lewis R. Bassford*, PRODUCTION PROJECT MANAGER; *Carol R. Curtis*, SENIOR PRODUCTION STAFF ASSISTANT

White House staff members who assisted in the preparation of this edition: *Rex Scouten*, CURATOR; *Betty Monkman*, ASSOCIATE CURATOR; *William Allman, Lydia Barker*, RESEARCH.

"The Avenue in the Rain," painted in 1917, is one of Childe Hassam's many studies of New York City's Fifth Avenue during a shower. It hangs in the West Wing of the White House.
FRONT COVER: *In autumn chrysanthemums encircle the fountain on the North Lawn.*
BACK COVER: *Illuminated at night, fountains splash before the South Portico.*

All objects of art and furniture pictured in this book belong to the White House Collection, unless otherwise noted.

FOREWORD

America's White House bears the stamp of every President. George Washington chose the site and approved the simple dignity of the architectural design. The building, begun in 1792, was still incomplete in 1800 when the first residents, John and Abigail Adams, moved in. Soon they, too, put their mark on it, as would each succeeding First Family.

To the throngs of visitors now passing through the White House, the tour offers glimpses of the lives and times of all the Presidents and their families. Their portraits adorn the walls and look out, here and there, on some of the same furnishings they themselves once used.

This official guide is in its 16th edition. The first one, which appeared in 1962, was planned by Mrs. John F. Kennedy to help visitors, as she put it, "sort out the impressions received on an often crowded visit." At that time, Congress—in line with Mrs. Kennedy's overall renovation project—had voted legislation to preserve the priceless possessions of the White House. Additionally, the nonprofit White House Historical Association had been formed to enhance understanding and appreciation of the Executive Mansion.

One of the first tasks of the Historical Association was to publish the guidebook, with the cooperation of the National Geographic Society, which provided the photographic and editorial staffs as a public service. All net proceeds from its sale are used to acquire furnishings and works of art linked with past Presidents and the White House, as well as to support related publications and restoration programs.

The Association has been aided by private donations that include superb examples of Federal-period furniture and several pieces from a state service ordered by President Monroe.

As an officer of both the White House Historical Association and the National Geographic Society, I am proud to have had a part in the White House projects since their beginning. This sentiment was shared by my colleague, the late Melville Bell Grosvenor, who, as Editor of National Geographic, was largely responsible for our participation. He enlisted the aid of Robert L. Breeden, now Senior Vice President for Publications and Educational Media, and Donald J. Crump, Director of the Special Publications Division. Together with their staff, they have produced the guide's many editions.

President and Mrs. Reagan take pleasure in welcoming each and every visitor to this house, and hope that they may find equal enjoyment in rediscovering American history at this national center of political, social, and family life.

Melvin M. Payne

Melvin M. Payne
Chairman and Chief Executive Officer, Board of Directors
White House Historical Association

Welcome!

My husband and I are delighted that you are visiting the White House today. In welcoming you, we feel a little like the tenants greeting the landlord, because this house and its history truly belong to all Americans.

Sometimes when walking down these halls, I am almost overcome with history when I realize that every President except George Washington has lived here. As you walk through, you can imagine President Lincoln looking thoughtfully out a window or President Jefferson striding down a corridor.

Not only have the residents changed over the years, but so also has the house itself. Laundry doesn't hang to dry in the East Room as it did during Abigail Adams's day. And Teddy Roosevelt's moose head no longer stares down from the wall of the State Dining Room on distinguished guests and foreign dignitaries.

Yet, whatever the changes from one administration to the next, the White House always maintains its character and dignity. This wonderful, historic house symbolizes the continuity of our democracy from generation to generation. I am glad you could visit the White House and renew your ties to America's heritage.

Nancy Reagan

Nancy Reagan

CONTENTS

I

A GUIDE TO
THE MANSION

More than a million visitors go through the White House every year, making it the most frequently toured home in this country. The only residence of a head of state open to the public on a regular basis free of charge, the White House is a museum of American history—with portraits of Presidents and First Ladies, works by some of America's finest artists, antique furniture in period settings, and memorabilia of historic importance. It is also the home and office of the President of the United States, where the pressing business of government is being conducted even as tourists visit nearby, admiring the mansion's many treasures from the past.

A painting on pages 102-3 of this book indicates the route of the tour through the White House and the locations of the most important rooms. Each tour begins in the wood-paneled East Wing Lobby and continues along the Ground Floor Corridor, up the wide marble staircase, and through the elegant rooms of the State Floor. Portraits of recent Presidents hang in the North Entrance, through which visitors pass as they leave the White House.

The first part of this book, "A Guide to the Mansion," describes, with historical notes, rooms open to the public and many that are not—some of the private family rooms on the second floor and the Presidential offices in the West Wing. The second part, "The Changing White House," traces, in illustrations and in words, the history of the mansion from its inception on the drawing board of architect James Hoban in 1792 through its many renovations.

Curving walk and driveway—shaded in spring by flowering magnolia—lead to the covered entranceway of the East Wing of the White House. Public tours of the Executive Mansion begin in the East Wing Lobby.

THE EAST COLONNADE

The Jacqueline Kennedy Garden on the east side of the White House serves primarily as an informal reception area for the First Lady. Flowering trees, shrubs, herbs, and colorful plantings that change with the seasons surround a rectangular lawn. A holly osmanthus hedge and a row of lindens provide shade for the colonnade that connects the East Wing with the mansion.

Most visitors to the White House enter through the East Wing Lobby, then proceed through the Garden Room to the glass-enclosed colonnade that leads to the Ground Floor of the White House. In the Lobby, built in 1942, hang portraits of First Ladies. The painting of Mrs. John Tyler was the first portrait of the wife of a President acquired for the White House Collection. Mrs. Grover Cleveland, Mrs. Harry S. Truman, and Mrs. Dwight D. Eisenhower are also represented here.

At the end of the hall and up a few steps is the Garden Room. To the right is the entrance to the colonnade, which was constructed in 1902 on the foundations of the original pavilion built by Thomas Jefferson and removed in 1869. Prior to 1857, a greenhouse was located in this area. Along the colonnade visitors have a view of the Jacqueline Kennedy Garden, so named by Lady Bird Johnson in 1965.

A massive bronze bust of Abraham Lincoln by Gutzon Borglum, the sculptor of Mount Rushmore, rests in a wall niche at the east end of the colonnade. At the west end, just before the entry to the Ground Floor, is a foyer in which hang portraits of Presidents. The marble bust of Christopher Columbus displayed here was bought by President James Monroe in 1817 from the son of George Washington's secretary, Tobias Lear.

Above: A bronze inkstand, gift of a descendant of its original owner, Thomas Jefferson, is one of many small objects of historic interest that have been displayed in changing exhibits along the colonnade. Julia Gardiner Tyler (left) suggested a First Lady portrait collection to President Andrew Johnson. To begin the tradition, she donated a portrait of herself, painted by Francisco Anelli in 1848.

GROUND FLOOR CORRIDOR

Until 1902 the Ground Floor Corridor and the rooms opening off of it were used as a work area. When Abraham Lincoln arrived at the White House in 1861, an aide recalled, the basement had "the air of an old and unsuccessful hotel." Even in the cold weather it reminded you "of old country taverns, if not of something you have smelled in the edge of some swamp."

Checking structural conditions in 1902, the New York architectural firm of McKim, Mead & White found that James Hoban's "fine, groined arches . . . had been cut into in all directions" to hold pipes. The furnace room jutted into the corridor; heat mains and a fresh-air duct hung from the ceiling. As a result of the 1902 renovation and extensive remodeling during the Truman Administration, Hoban's elegant vaulted ceiling was restored to its clean simplicity and the hall transformed by walls and floors of marble, antique furniture, and works of art.

Selected pieces of White House china are now displayed in a Baltimore Sheraton-style breakfront bookcase. Two sculptures with Western themes by Frederic Remington and Charles Russell flank the entrance from the East Foyer.

The custom of hanging portraits of First Ladies in this area dates from 1902 when Mrs. Theodore Roosevelt wrote to Charles McKim asking that "all the ladies of the White House, including myself," be relegated to "the downstairs corridor. . . ." Traditionally, portraits of recent First Ladies have been displayed on either side of the entrance to the Diplomatic Reception Room. On the right is Felix de Cossio's 1977 portrait of Elizabeth Bloomer Ford and on the left is Rosalynn Smith Carter, painted in 1984 by George Augusta. Aaron Shikler's 1970 portrait of Jacqueline Kennedy Onassis hangs at the east end of the corridor. Three Regency bronze-and-crystal chandeliers light the gallery.

Under the portraits are two similar pier tables (originally designed to fit into a pier, or space between two openings), one labeled by the New York cabinetmaker Charles-Honoré Lannuier and the other attributed to him. Flanking these are four lattice-back chairs attributed to the workshop of Samuel McIntire of Salem, Massachusetts. Bronze figures of Henry Clay and Daniel Webster, by Thomas Ball, are displayed beside the doorway. Directly across the hall are two bronze heads: British Prime Minister Winston Churchill by Jacob Epstein and President Dwight D. Eisenhower by Nison Tregor.

At the west end of the corridor are portraits of Claudia "Lady Bird" Johnson, Patricia Ryan Nixon, and Caroline Scott Harrison. Mrs. Harrison, a talented amateur artist, designed the Harrison china now displayed in the China Room and in the Family Dining Room.

The Ground Floor Corridor provides an elegant gallery for visitors on their way to the State Floor. An early Presidential seal, embedded in the North Entrance floor in 1902, was moved to the wall above the doorway to the Diplomatic Reception Room during the Truman renovation of 1948-52.

The Sheraton-style breakfront bookcase, made in Baltimore in the period 1800-10, displays a selection of Presidential china. During the administration of Theodore Roosevelt, the Ground Floor Corridor was lined with cabinets containing the White House china collection, which was started by Caroline Scott Harrison in 1889 and greatly expanded by Mrs. Roosevelt. It had grown so large by 1917 that Edith Galt Wilson had it placed in a special area known today as the China Room. On the top shelf, center, stand plates used by George Washington at Mount Vernon; the shelf below displays Lincoln china.

Patricia Ryan Nixon sat for Henriette Wyeth Hurd at the former Nixon home in San Clemente, California, in 1978. As First Lady, she encouraged volunteer service and initiated Christmas candlelight tours of the White House and spring and fall garden tours for the public. She played an active role in refurbishing the mansion and acquiring many paintings and decorative art objects for the collection.

New York artist Aaron Shikler painted this portrait of Jacqueline Kennedy Onassis in 1970; her New York apartment provides the background. As First Lady to John F. Kennedy, she was particularly concerned with historic restoration of the White House to reflect the times and tastes of the families who have lived there. She established a Fine Arts Committee to acquire period furnishings and works of art, and sponsored the creation of the White House Historical Association.

In his portrait of Elizabeth Bloomer Ford, painted in 1977 at the Fords' home in Vail, Colorado, Felix de Cossio captures her poise and forthrightness as First Lady. Not hesitating to state her views publicly, she strongly supported the Equal Rights Amendment.

While visiting Washington in 1984, Rosalynn Carter posed for artist George Augusta in historic Blair House, across the street from the White House. As First Lady, she showed great interest in programs to aid the mentally ill.

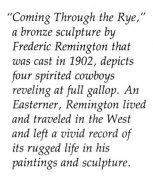

"Coming Through the Rye," a bronze sculpture by Frederic Remington that was cast in 1902, depicts four spirited cowboys reveling at full gallop. An Easterner, Remington lived and traveled in the West and left a vivid record of its rugged life in his paintings and sculpture.

THE LIBRARY

The Library was completely redecorated in 1962 as a "painted" room typical of the early 1800's, and was refurbished again in 1976. The paneling, now a soft gray color, dates from the Truman renovation of 1948-52. Old timber removed when the mansion was stripped to a shell was made into paneling for various ground-floor rooms. Over the mantel hangs a Gilbert Stuart portrait of George Washington, painted about 1805, which was donated to the White House in 1949. Right: portraits by Charles Bird King of Indian emissaries who visited the mansion in 1821— Hayn-Hudjihini, or "Eagle of Delight," of the Oto Tribe, who contracted measles during her visit and died shortly after she returned home, and Sharitarish, or "Wicked Chief," of the Pawnee Tribe.

"Tubs, Buckets and a variety of Lumber" cluttered Room 17 of the basement in February 1801, according to the first official White House inventory. The room served mainly as a laundry area until Theodore Roosevelt's renovation of the Ground Floor in 1902, when it was designated a "Gentlemen's Ante-room." In 1937, it was remodeled as a library, and in 1961 a committee was appointed to select works representative of a full spectrum of American thought and tradition for the use of the President, his family, and his staff. This wide-ranging collection is still being augmented with Presidential biographies and papers.

The Library is furnished in the style of the late Federal period (1800-20) with most of the pieces attributed to the New York cabinetmaker Duncan Phyfe. It is less formal than the rooms of the State Floor and is often used for small teas and meetings. The soft gray and rose tones of the paneling are complemented by a mid-19th-century Tabriz rug. The gilded wood chandelier with a painted red band was made about 1800 and belonged to the family of James Fenimore Cooper, author of *The Last of the Mohicans* and other classics.

An unusual Federal-period looking glass, acquired in 1971, hangs on the north wall between the windows. The top portion contains a rare example of églomisé painting—reverse painting on glass—of an American eagle bearing in its talons the motto from the Great Seal of the United States. The looking glass, made in New York in the early 19th century, has an architectural frame of gilded wood. Below the looking glass is one of a pair of Phyfe caned settees. The other settee, flanked by two similar sewing or work tables, stands against the south wall opposite the windows. In front of the windows are two of six matching Phyfe "cross-bannister" chairs with caned seats covered by cushions. The drum table in the center of the room is also attributed to Phyfe.

The neoclassical mantel on the west wall, from a house in Salem, Massachusetts, was carved by Samuel McIntire, master craftsman of that town. To the right of the fireplace is a Massachusetts Sheraton-style armchair; to the left is a Phyfe card table and an armchair matching the Phyfe side chairs flanking the east door. This set is finely carved in leaf and rosette motifs.

On the mantel rests a pair of English silver-plate Argand lamps, a gift of the Marquis de Lafayette to Gen. Henry Knox, Secretary of War in Washington's Cabinet. Such lamps, named after their Swiss inventor, Aimé Argand, were a major innovation; George Washington ordered some in 1790, noting that by report they "consume their own smoke . . . give more light, and are cheaper than candles."

One of the many Athenaeum portraits of George Washington by Gilbert Stuart hangs over the mantel. Stuart painted three portraits of Washington from life, the Vaughan portrait (1795), now in the National Gallery of Art; the full-length Lansdowne portrait (1796), owned by the Earl of Rosebery and on loan to the National Portrait Gallery; and the Athenaeum portrait (1796), which was acquired in 1876 by the Boston Athenaeum and is now owned jointly by the National Portrait Gallery

The lighthouse clock, patented in 1822 by Simon Willard of Roxbury, Massachusetts, has a fragile glass dome with an alarm bell inside. The medallion on the mahogany base shows the Marquis de Lafayette. Below: an Argand lamp presented by Lafayette to Gen. Henry Knox, his friend and comrade-in-arms.

and the Museum of Fine Arts in Boston. Gilbert Stuart kept the Athenaeum portrait throughout his life and made well over 50 replicas of it for patriotic Americans. The portrait in the Library was painted for a Baltimore family and, like all the copies, varies slightly from the original. Stuart also made copies of the Lansdowne portrait, one of which hangs in the East Room.

One of the bookshelves displays an unusual lighthouse clock made by Simon Willard. A medallion in its base bears a likeness of the Marquis de Lafayette. Hanging in the corner of the room is a long wooden pole that unfolds to form a narrow ladder. Such ladders were used in England as library steps; the one in this room is a reproduction of an 18th-century version. Called "machan" or "howdah" ladders, they were used in India for entering hunting blinds or for mounting and dismounting elephants. Machan derives from the Indian word for scaffolding, and a howdah is the covered seat or pavilion on an elephant's back.

Four portraits of American Indians by Charles Bird King flank the east door, and a fifth hangs over the entrance to the corridor. The paintings, given to the White House in 1962, are King's own copies from a set of eight portraits commissioned in 1821 for the American Indian archives, then located in Georgetown. The originals, which were in the Smithsonian Institution, were destroyed by fire in 1865. The federal government, fearing that westward expansion would be met by violent opposition from the powerful and militant tribes of the Great Plains, invited a number of Indian leaders to visit the nation's most important cities and forts and to meet their "Great Father," the President. Government officials hoped to overawe these Indians with an impressive show of military strength, luxurious gifts, and elaborate ceremony.

When the Indians arrived in Washington, merchants fitted them out in military finery for an audience with President James Monroe. They were formally received by the President in the Red Room on February 4, 1822. With the help of interpreters, he thanked them for coming, spoke of the white man's strength and the blessings of peace, and offered to send missionaries to instruct them in Christianity and agriculture. The chiefs, impressed but feeling ill-at-ease in their new clothes, gravely replied that they admired the things they had seen but preferred their own life of trapping beaver and hunting buffalo. Sharitarish, their leader, added: " . . . we have plenty of land, if you will keep your people off it."

Each speaker laid a gift at the President's feet: moccasins, feathered headdresses, buffalo robes, and peace pipes. Before the party moved to the Blue Room for cake and wine, Sharitarish expressed the hope that Monroe would order the presents kept "in some conspicuous part of your lodge, so that when we are gone . . . if our children should visit this place, as we do now, they may see and recognize with pleasure the deposits of their fathers, and reflect on the times that are past." The gifts were unfortunately lost long ago, and efforts to avoid fighting were finally unsuccessful.

THE VERMEIL ROOM

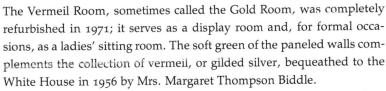

"Morning on the Seine" (left), by Claude Monet, is one of a series of 18 similar views painted by the artist in 1897 to record the changing effects of light and color. A vermeil wine cooler (far left), made in London in 1823 by Philip Rundell, has as its handles classical figures reaching for grapes from an arbor.

The Vermeil Room, sometimes called the Gold Room, was completely refurbished in 1971; it serves as a display room and, for formal occasions, as a ladies' sitting room. The soft green of the paneled walls complements the collection of vermeil, or gilded silver, bequeathed to the White House in 1956 by Mrs. Margaret Thompson Biddle.

The vermeil collection contains pieces from different services and includes the work of English Regency silversmith Paul Storr (1771-1844) and French Empire silversmith Jean-Baptiste-Claude Odiot (1763-1850). The Biddle flatware and some of the platters are used on state occasions with reproductions of the gilt flatware ordered by Monroe in 1817.

The green satin draperies are of early 19th-century design. The rug is a Turkish Hereke of about 1860, chosen for its pale-green background and gold silk highlights. The French neoclassical mantel, dating from about 1830 and installed in 1962, features two draped female figures in relief, derived from caryatids, free-standing figures sometimes used as columns in Greek architecture.

To the left of the window stands a classical pier table made in New York about 1810, which bears the label of its maker, Charles-Honoré Lannuier. Hanging above it, Douglas Chandor's 1949 portrait of Eleanor Roosevelt at age 65 conveys her many moods and boundless energy. Mrs. Roosevelt, reluctant to pose, inscribed the canvas: "A trial made pleasant by the painter."

Matching tables under the display niches in the west wall are in the American Empire style and are attributed to the New York workshop of Lannuier. A pair of settees made in Massachusetts in the early 19th century flanks the fireplace. The oil painting above the mantel, "Morning on the Seine," completed in 1897 by the French Impressionist Claude Monet, was given to the White House by the Kennedy family in 1963 in memory of President John F. Kennedy.

To the left of the doorway is a drawing by Jean-Honoré Fragonard, "The Apotheosis [or deification] of Franklin," executed in 1778 while Benjamin Franklin was in France to win support for the colonists' struggle against the British. This drawing, a classical allegory, depicts a laurel-crowned Franklin with his right hand invoking Athena to protect the seated figure of America and his left hand encouraging Mars to strike down Avarice and Tyranny in the foreground.

Gilbert Stuart's 1804 portrait of Mrs. Richard Cutts, Dolley Madison's sister, hangs on the north wall, along with a portrait of Benjamin Henry Latrobe by Charles Willson Peale. Peale painted Latrobe from life in about 1804, a year after the architect had been named "Surveyor of the Public Buildings" by President Thomas Jefferson.

THE CHINA ROOM

The "Presidential Collection Room," now the China Room, was designated by Mrs. Woodrow Wilson in 1917 to display the growing collection of White House china. The room was redecorated in 1970, retaining the traditional red color scheme determined by the portrait of Mrs. Calvin Coolidge—painted by Howard Chandler Christy in 1924. President Coolidge, who was scheduled to sit for Christy, was too occupied that day with events concerning the Teapot Dome oil scandal. So the President postponed his appointment, and Mrs. Coolidge posed instead. The

red theme continues in the velvet-lined cabinets, silk taffeta draperies,
and an English rug of about 1850, handwoven in the Savonnerie manner.
The cut-glass chandelier, made about 1800, is in the English Regency
style. The two American chairs flanking the mantel, called "Martha
Washington" or "lolling" chairs, were made in the early 19th
century. The painting "View on the Mississippi, Fifty-Seven Miles Below
St. Anthony Falls, Minneapolis," which hangs above the mantel, was completed
by Ferdinand Richardt in 1858—the year Minnesota achieved statehood.

Almost every past President is represented in the China Room either by state or family china or glassware. The collection is arranged chronologically, beginning to the right of the fireplace.

Even the earliest Presidents received government funds to purchase state china. However, by a special clause in the appropriation bills, "decayed furnishings" could be sold and the proceeds used to buy replacements. Such "furnishings" included state china, and during the 19th century the cupboards were frequently swept clean and the contents carted off to auction. The money could then be used to order a new china service that better suited the President and his family. Much china, deemed unusable because of cracks or other damage, was given away. Large amounts were also lost through breakage. Thousands of dollars' worth of china and glass were broken at the celebration following Andrew Jackson's inauguration, for example. Unruly crowds thronged the White House trying to catch a glimpse of the new President, who was finally forced to escape and spend the night at a boardinghouse.

Obviously, not much historical importance was attached to White House china during the first hundred years of the Presidency. In 1889, however, Mrs. Benjamin Harrison started to collect pieces from previous administrations, and her project was continued by Mrs. William McKinley. The collection was greatly expanded by Mrs. Theodore Roosevelt, who strongly opposed the sale of any White House china. She also stopped the practice of giving away or selling damaged china; it was broken and scattered into the Potomac River instead.

Many Presidents have chosen not to order new state china, either because it was not needed or because the appropriation was used for other things. Presidents who use their personal china in the White House take it with them when they leave; most of such pieces in the collection have been acquired from their descendants or at auction.

Until the administration of Woodrow Wilson all Presidential china was produced outside the United States—usually in France or England. Patriotic symbols, especially the American eagle, frequently appear in the china designs. The service chosen by Mrs. Lyndon B. Johnson also features American wild flowers. A new state china pattern selected by Mrs. Ronald Reagan was donated to the White House in 1982; a wide red border overlaid with gold latticework and edged with gold decorates the service plates.

For unabashed assertion of national pride, no china could outshine the exuberant Hayes service; purchased in 1879, it portrays American flora and fauna. The game platter with a strutting wild turkey is one of a series of painted and sculpted plates decorated with wild animals, fish, fruits, and vegetables. When the china first appeared at a state dinner, according to one report, it formed "the most conspicuous part of the furniture of the table."

Above: a serving platter from the flamboyant Hayes china, made in France by Haviland & Co. Early Presidential family china (bottom right): a Sèvres tureen owned by John and Abigail Adams; a Chinese export porcelain sugar bowl from Martha Washington's monogrammed personal china; a French cup and saucer, part of a service purchased by James Madison from James Monroe. Dolley Madison designed the monogram.

Below: plates from four state services. The Lyndon B. Johnson china, made by Castleton China, Inc., of Pennsylvania, features a border of flowers and an American eagle derived from the eagle on an amaranth-rimmed plate from Monroe's French Dagoty service. Bordered in navy and gold, Wilson's china, ordered from Lenox of New Jersey, was the first state service made in the United States. The Reagan service also came from Lenox; an etched gold band and red border overlaid by gold latticework surround an ivory center with raised gold Presidential seal.

Above: Classical figures adorn a rococo-revival punch bowl from the Franklin Pierce Administration. Mrs. Benjamin Harrison found the bowl in the White House attic and had it mended and put on display as a piece of historical White House china.

THE DIPLOMATIC RECEPTION ROOM

The Diplomatic Reception Room, once used as a boiler and furnace room, is now furnished as a drawing room of the early 19th century. It serves principally as an entrance to the White House from the South Grounds for the family and for new ambassadors arriving to present their credentials to the President.

In 1960, during the Eisenhower Administration, the Diplomatic Reception Room was furnished in the styles of the Federal period (1790-1820) with many fine examples of the craftsmanship of New York and New England cabinetmakers. The gold-and-white color scheme was chosen at the same time. An oval rug was woven in the Aubusson manner specially for this room; it has emblems of the 50 states incorporated into the border.

Additional furniture was placed in the room in 1961 and the striking panoramic wallpaper added. The paper, called "Scenic America," was first printed in 1834 by Jean Zuber et Cie in Rixheim, Alsace. (Wallpaper was widely used in 19th-century America and covered many of the White House walls at that time.) The scenes, based on engravings of the 1820's, show American landscapes that were particularly admired by Europeans. Starting to the left of the doorway as you enter from the Ground Floor Corridor are the Natural Bridge of Virginia, Niagara Falls, New York Bay, West Point, and Boston Harbor. The wallpaper was printed with wood blocks on small sheets of paper which were then glued together into panels. The views are all somewhat fanciful; Boston Harbor is believed to be the most accurate.

In 1971 a Regency chandelier was added, and a new carpet was woven because the original had become worn (this, in turn, was replaced in 1983). The sofa, Pembroke table, and the armchair on the right are in the Hepplewhite style. The sweeping curved back and graceful reverse-curve arm supports of the sofa are typical Hepplewhite designs. The card tables flanking the sofa and the other armchair are in the Sheraton style. An Annapolis secretary bearing the label of John Shaw and dated 1797 was moved into this room in 1974.

Near the doorway to the South Grounds are a pair of Sheraton-style settees and two matching chairs attributed to the New York workshop of Slover and Taylor. To the right of the door stands a mahogany tall-case clock with musical chimes and works by Effingham Embree of New York. Its bonnet bears a patriotic eagle motif in wood inlay.

One of the three oval rooms in the White House proper, the Diplomatic Reception Room exhibits American Federal-period furniture. The room provides a handsome entrance for diplomats arriving to present credentials.

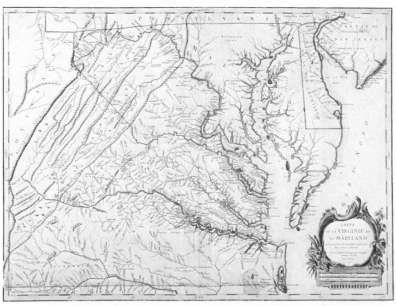

THE MAP ROOM

The Map Room, used by President Franklin D. Roosevelt as a situation room from which to follow the course of World War II, now serves as a private meeting room for the President and First Lady. It was redecorated in 1970 as a reception room in the Chippendale style, which flourished in America during the last half of the 18th century.

Named after the English furniture designer Thomas Chippendale, this style combines the graceful lines of Queen Anne furniture with more elaborate rococo, Gothic, and Chinese carved motifs. Cabinetmakers in Massachusetts and Rhode Island adapted the Chippendale style to a unique American furniture treatment termed "blockfront," in which the central of three vertical panels of a piece of furniture is recessed. A blockfront chest, made in Massachusetts about 1760, stands to the left of the window; to the right is a blockfront slant-top desk produced between 1760 and 1765 and bearing the carved-shell motif that was characteristic of the Townsends and Goddards, allied families of cabinetmakers from Newport, Rhode Island.

Notable among the Chippendale-style pieces from Philadelphia in the room are a side chair carrying the label of James Gillingham and three attributed to him, an elaborately carved highboy, and a library table with Chinese-style fretwork along its apron. On a Philadelphia Chippendale chest to the right of the mantel rests a medicine chest that belonged to James Madison. Taken from the White House by a British soldier in 1814, it was returned in 1939 by one of his descendants.

On the blockfront desk is a silver pitcher once owned by President Martin Van Buren. Hanging above the desk is a portrait of Benjamin Franklin completed in 1759 in London by Benjamin Wilson. It was removed from Franklin's house in Philadelphia during the American Revolution by the British officer John André. André was later hanged as a spy by the Americans for his role as intermediary in Gen. Benedict Arnold's plot to betray West Point to the British in 1780. Gen. Charles Grey (later the first Earl Grey), once André's commanding officer, took the painting back to England. In 1906 the fourth Earl Grey returned the portrait in honor of the bicentennial of Franklin's birth.

The Map Room contains three landscapes by artists of the Hudson River School. "Autumn Landscape on the Hudson River," painted by Jasper Cropsey in 1876, hangs above the mantel. Across the room is "Lake Among the Hills," painted by William M. Hart in 1858. "Tending Cows and Sheep," painted by Alvan Fisher in 1854, faces the windows.

The rug, a brilliantly colored Heriz, is one of several kinds of Persian rugs popular during the 19th century. The cut-glass chandelier, made in England about 1765, has rare star pendants.

Brightly colored Heriz rug and Chippendale-style furniture decorate the Map Room. Left: Rare 1775 French version of a map charted by colonial surveyors Joshua Fry and Peter Jefferson (Thomas Jefferson's father) hangs on the east wall, covering a case of current world maps presented by the National Geographic Society.

THE
NORTH
ENTRANCE

The large Entrance Hall and the Cross Hall formed part of James Hoban's original plans for the White House. The basic design has not been altered, although modifications have been made during various renovations. During the 19th century two principal stairways led to the second floor. The Grand Staircase at the west end of the Cross Hall (see page 145) was removed in 1902 to increase the size of the State Dining Room. At the same time, the remaining stairway, opening into the Cross Hall, was enlarged. During the 1948-52 renovation, this stairway was repositioned to open into the Entrance Hall.

The Cross Hall, with marble walls and floors added during the Truman renovation, is lighted by two Adam-style cut-glass chandeliers made in London about 1790. The decorative plaster ceiling insets and the bronze light standards date from the Theodore Roosevelt renovation of 1902. A French settee once owned by President Monroe stands beneath the 1970 portrait of John F. Kennedy by Aaron Shikler.

Other Presidential portraits hang at the east end of the Cross Hall: Lyndon B. Johnson by Elizabeth Shoumatoff, Richard M. Nixon by J. Anthony Wills, and Jimmy Carter by Herbert E. Abrams. A portrait of President Truman, painted by Greta Kempton, hangs at the west end of the hall. Two marble busts are displayed in niches along the south wall: American diplomat and poet Joel Barlow by Jean-Antoine Houdon and George Washington after Houdon.

The Cross Hall has not always had this look of elegant simplicity. In 1865 an inventory dismissed its furnishings as "all pretty common." Perhaps its most spectacular alteration occurred in 1882 when President Arthur called on Louis C. Tiffany of New York to redecorate the mansion. A stained-glass screen, reaching from floor to ceiling, was placed between the columns to divide the Cross Hall from the Entrance Hall (see pages 130-31). One observer remarked: "The light coming through the partition of wrinkled stained glass mosaic makes a marvelously rich and gorgeous effect, falling upon the gilded niches where stand dwarf palmetto trees, the silvery network of the ceiling, and the sumptuous furniture. . . ." In these lavish surroundings the Grover Clevelands held their last dinner for the Diplomatic Corps, by then far too large for the State Dining Room. The McKinleys also gave dinners here. Apparently, the Tiffany screen did not block the flow of cold air from the North Entrance very effectively: "A gale roared through the improvised banquet hall whenever the front door was opened," writes historian Margaret Leech, "and the floor was so cold that the divans were robbed of cushions to make footstools for the ladies."

Until 1902, when the President's second-floor offices were moved to

The Cross Hall (above), separated from the Entrance Hall by the colonnade constructed after Hoban's original design, extends between the State Dining Room and the East Room. A life portrait of Dwight D. Eisenhower (opposite), painted by J. Anthony Wills in 1967, hangs in the Entrance Hall. A marble bust of American diplomat and poet Joel Barlow, by Jean-Antoine Houdon, (opposite, right) is displayed in a niche beyond the flags.

The portrait of Gerald R. Ford, by Everett Raymond Kinstler, hangs on the west wall of the Entrance Hall. President Ford sat for the painting in his home in Vail, Colorado, in July 1977, six months after he left office.

Herbert E. Abrams painted the portrait of Jimmy Carter in Plains, Georgia, in 1982. Displayed in the Cross Hall, it depicts Carter seated in an armchair from the Red Room.

THE NORTH ENTRANCE

Presidential portraits, a cut-glass chandelier, and red carpet on marble steps decorate the main stairway, the elegant passage between the Family and State Floors. On state occasions the President and First Lady usually escort official visitors down the grand staircase to the Entrance Hall, where they pose for photographers.

the newly built West Wing, the Entrance Hall served as a reception area and as a busy passageway. The furnishings were, by necessity, utilitarian and, judging from the inventories, consistently worn.

The Entrance Hall is seen by visitors as they leave the White House. It is set off from the Cross Hall by the Hoban-designed colonnade and is decorated in the same style. Its furnishings include a French pier table purchased by Monroe in 1817 and a pair of French settees with carved mahogany swans' heads. A suite of early 19th-century gilded furniture in the French Empire style, used by President Monroe, was added to the halls in 1973. By tradition, portraits of recent Presidents hang in the Entrance and Cross Halls; the portraits of Gerald R. Ford and Dwight D. Eisenhower now hang on the west and east walls of the Entrance Hall.

The main stairway is often used on ceremonial occasions. Before state dinners, the President greets his guests of honor in the Yellow Oval Room; then they descend the stairs to the East Room where the other guests are gathered. Along the stairway hang portraits of 20th-century Presidents, including Franklin D. Roosevelt by Frank O. Salisbury, Woodrow Wilson by F. Graham Cootes, Warren G. Harding by F. Luis Mora, and William McKinley by Harriet S. Murphy; a portrait of Mrs. William Howard Taft by Bror Kronstrand is also in the stairway. Above the American pier table on the stair landing is a portrait of Herbert Hoover by Elmer W. Greene.

THE EAST ROOM

The East Room, scene of many historic White House events, was designated by Hoban as the "Public Audience Room." It normally contains little furniture and traditionally is used for large gatherings of many different kinds, including dances, after-dinner entertainments, concerts, weddings, funerals, award presentations, press conferences, and bill-signing ceremonies.

Today the East Room retains the late 18th-century classical style to which it was restored by architects McKim, Mead & White during the Roosevelt renovation of 1902. An oak floor of Fontainebleau parquetry was installed at that time as were the bronze electric-light standards, upholstered benches, and three Bohemian cut-glass chandeliers. The walls were paneled in wood with classical fluted pilasters and eight relief insets illustrating Aesop's fables. The paneling was painted white, and delicate plaster decoration was added to the ceiling.

The room was originally designed with two fireplaces in the west wall and five windows in the east wall. Latrobe's 1807 plan to wall in four of the five windows was adopted in the first quarter of the 19th century, and two new fireplaces were added. New marble mantels were installed over the four fireplaces during the Truman renovation of 1948-52. A gold-and-white color scheme was chosen by Mrs. Theodore Roosevelt, although Charles McKim originally had envisioned crimson draperies for this room. Red draperies were substituted during the Franklin D. Roosevelt Administration, but the Truman renovation returned the East Room to the gold-and-white theme. In 1983 gold damask draperies of French fabric were hung at the windows.

The Steinway grand piano with gilt American eagle supports was designed by Eric Gugler and was given to the White House in 1938 by the manufacturer. It is decorated with gilt stenciling by Dunbar Beck.

The full-length portrait of George Washington that hangs in the East Room is one of several replicas made by Gilbert Stuart of his original "Lansdowne" portrait. It is the only object known to have remained in the White House since 1800—except for a period after the British burned the mansion during the War of 1812.

Dolley Madison had refused to abandon the portrait as she fled; she wrote to her sister on the day of the fire: "Our kind friend, Mr. Carroll, has come to hasten my departure, and is in a very bad humor with me because I insist on waiting until the large picture of Gen. Washington is

The East Room, largest and most formal of the state reception rooms, remained unfinished until 1829. The present classical decor dates largely from the 1902 renovation; George Washington's portrait hangs on the east wall.

secured, and it requires to be unscrewed from the wall. This process was found too tedious for these perilous moments; I have ordered the frame to be broken, and the canvas taken out; it is done,—and the precious portrait placed in the hands of two gentlemen of New York, for safe keeping. And now, dear sister, I must leave this house, or the retreating army will make me a prisoner in it, by filling up the road I am directed to take. . . ." Her efforts were successful, and the portrait was returned to the White House when the rebuilding was completed. The companion portrait of Martha Washington was painted by Eliphalet F. Andrews in 1878.

Although intended by Hoban to be the most elegant of the state reception rooms, the East Room remained unfinished for 29 years. It was here that the John Adams family, first occupants of the White House, dried their laundry, presumably with the help of two "Ten Plate" stoves listed in an inventory of February 26, 1801.

Thomas Jefferson partitioned the space to create two rooms for his secretary, Meriwether Lewis—later co-leader of the Lewis and Clark expedition—who had to move his quarters when the East Room ceiling fell in. Architect Benjamin Latrobe, appointed by Jefferson as Surveyor of Public Buildings, noted on a floor plan executed in 1803: "Public Audience Chamber—entirely unfinished, the ceiling has given way." Jefferson's inventory of 1809 lists "34 armed Chairs black and Gold" in the "Large Unfinished Room," and "1 Table & Kettles for washing Tumblers," indicating that the room may have been used as a makeshift butler's pantry as well as a storage area. James Madison met with his Cabinet in the south end of the East Room; but whatever furnishings the room might have contained were destroyed in the fire of 1814, and no record of them remains.

After the fire, restoration of the White House included work on the "principal drawing room"; by November 21, 1818, Hoban reported that the floor had been laid, the walls and ceiling plastered, and the cornice, frieze, architrave, and decorative woodwork nearly finished. The appropriations, however, were not adequate to furnish the East Room properly. Four sofas and two dozen chairs were placed in the room, but their upholstery was unfinished (see page 119).

President John Quincy Adams opened the room to provide space for the large New Year's Day receptions during his term; the furniture remained unupholstered. It was not until 1829 that Andrew Jackson finally decorated the room in grand style, at a cost to the taxpayer of more than $9,000.

Jackson's purchases included "three 18-light" chandeliers with cut glass of "remarkable brilliancy," a "3-light centre lamp supported by female figures," eight "5-light" gilded wall brackets, and various table lamps. Four fireplaces were fitted with black-marble mantels with "Italian black and gold fronts"; four huge gilt-frame mirrors were placed above these mantels. Almost 500 yards of red-bordered Brussels carpet was purchased for the floor, and lemon-yellow paper covered the walls.

THE EAST ROOM

Two pairs of candelabra displayed on the mantels on the west wall were originally purchased in 1817 by President Monroe. Made of gilded bronze, they are thought to be the work of Pierre-Philippe Thomire, a French bronze caster.

A clergyman from New England found this "great levee apartment . . . truly magnificent," carefully noting the "light-blue satin-silk" on the sofas and chairs and the "white, blue, and light-yellow commingled" hues of the curtains. Even if the ladies of his party agreed that the rich carpet "needed the cleansing effect of tea-leaves," he concluded that: "On the whole it is a seat worthy of the people's idol."

During the Civil War years and the administration of Abraham Lincoln there was much activity in the East Room. At one time during the war Union troops occupied the room. In 1864 the East Room was the scene of a large reception given by President Lincoln in honor of Ulysses S. Grant shortly before his appointment as head of all the Union armies. In April of 1865 the East Room was again filled with people, but this time they were mourners surrounding the body of President Lincoln after he had been assassinated by John Wilkes Booth. Lincoln lay in state on a black-draped catafalque, much as he had foreseen in a dream a few weeks earlier. Seven Presidents have lain in state in the East Room, including John F. Kennedy in November 1963.

Furnishings in the East Room had become shabby and worn by the time General Grant became President. In 1873 a drastic renovation transformed the room into a salon decorated in the Victorian style (see page 124). The ceiling was divided into three sections with ornate false beams supported by gilded columns. Large gas chandeliers, patterned carpeting and wall coverings, heavy mirrors, and rich fabrics created what sometimes has been referred to as "steamboat palace" decor. In this setting President Grant's daughter, Nellie, was married in 1874 under a huge bell of roses. An elaborate wedding breakfast followed in the State Dining Room. The next wedding to take place in the East Room was that of Alice Roosevelt in 1906. By that time, the room had been restored to the classic simplicity of the late 18th century. The most recent wedding here was Lynda Johnson's in 1967.

Gilbert Stuart's 1797 portrait of George Washington was rescued by Dolley Madison shortly before the British burned the White House on August 24, 1814. The painting has been the property of the mansion since 1800.

When President Arthur redecorated the White House in 1882, Louis C. Tiffany found it necessary only to install silver paper on the ceiling of the East Room and to increase the number of potted plants. All of these heavy Victorian adornments were swept away in the 1902 restoration. During the Theodore Roosevelt Administration, this room became the scene of some rather unusual activities, including a wrestling match arranged to entertain some 50 to 60 guests of the President. The exuberant Roosevelt children are also known to have used the East Room for roller-skating.

THE
GREEN
ROOM

Although intended by Hoban to be the "Common Dining Room," the Green Room has served many purposes since the White House was first occupied in 1800. The inventory of February 1801 indicates that it was first used as a "Lodging Room." Thomas Jefferson, the second occupant of the White House, used it as a dining room with a "canvass floor cloth, painted Green," foreshadowing the present color scheme. James Madison made it a sitting room since his Cabinet met in the East Room next door, and the Monroes used it as the "Card Room" with two tables for the whist players among their guests.

When the Monroes, the first occupants of the White House after the fire of 1814, set about refurnishing the mansion, they decorated the room with green silks. With the next President, John Quincy Adams, came the name "Green Drawing Room" and a green drawing room it has remained, traditionally serving as a parlor for small teas and receptions and on occasion for formal dinners.

Not every President has chosen a green everyone liked. The shade that Andrew Jackson approved provoked unfavorable comment from the ladies; they found the color "odious . . . from the sallow look it imparts." Styles in the room changed as frequently as the tastes of the Presidents until the time of Theodore Roosevelt, when it was furnished with reproductions of early 19th-century American furniture. Not until the Coolidge Administration, however, was authentic Federal-period furniture placed in the room.

The Green Room was completely refurbished in 1971. Its walls were re-covered with the delicate green watered-silk fabric originally chosen by Mrs. Kennedy in 1962. Draperies of striped beige, green, and coral satin—a major part of the 1971 renovation—were carefully designed from a pattern shown in an early 19th-century periodical. The coral-and-gilt ornamental cornices are surmounted by a pair of hand-carved, gilded American eagles with outspread wings. The eagle, patriotic symbol of the United States, was one of the favored decorative motifs of the Federal period and appears in many forms in this room.

The carpet is a Turkish Hereke of 19th-century design, with a multi-colored pattern on a green field. This green background, sometimes found in small Muslim prayer rugs, is unusual in a rug of this size.

The cut-glass-and-ormolu chandelier, made in France in the early 19th century, was installed in the room in 1975. The plaster ceiling

The Green Room, a first-floor parlor, was completely refurbished in 1971. Its furniture, in the styles of the Federal period, includes many pieces attributed to the famous New York cabinetmaker Duncan Phyfe.

As wife of the Secretary of State, Louisa Catherine Adams posed for Gilbert Stuart in 1821, four years before her husband, John Quincy Adams, became President. This portrait is displayed in the Green Room (left). David Martin's 1767 portrait of a scholarly, aging Benjamin Franklin hangs over the mantel. "Farmyard in Winter" (below), painted by George H. Durrie in 1858, depicts a Connecticut farm of about 1825. The unusual work table (right), one of two flanking the mantel, has a hinged lid and sides that open to reveal trays and small compartments. It may have been designed for fine sewing or possibly for painting miniatures. The

Argand lamp, named after its Swiss inventor Aimé Argand, was ingeniously designed with a tubular wick to burn brighter and cleaner than other lamps of the late 18th century.

medallion above the chandelier, adapted from designs of the Federal period, was installed in 1971.

In "a noble, or genteel house," wrote Thomas Sheraton, the English furniture designer, a drawing room "should possess all the elegance embellishments can give." Most of the furnishings now in the Green Room date from the years 1800-15, the period of Sheraton's greatest influence on American decor. Many of the pieces are attributed to the New York workshop of the well-known Scottish-born cabinetmaker Duncan Phyfe, who enjoyed a reputation for fine design and excellence of craftsmanship.

Among the pieces attributed to the Phyfe workshop is the Sheraton secretary-bookcase, made about 1815, which stands between the windows on the south wall. The secretary has many details of Phyfe's work, including the richly figured mahogany veneers that contrast with the satinwood-faced drawers and pigeonholes inside its cylinder desk section. A collection of early 19th-century Chinese export porcelain in the Green Fitzhugh pattern, displayed on the shelves, features a sepia-and-gold American eagle with the motto from the Great Seal: *E Pluribus Unum*. Above the secretary hangs "Lighter Relieving a Steamboat Aground," painted by George Caleb Bingham in 1846-47, after he returned to Missouri from the East Coast and began depicting the scenes of everyday life for which he became best known. The New York armchair at the desk bears the signature of Lawrence Ackerman, one of Phyfe's upholsterers, on the seat frame. In the window niches is a pair of rare mahogany Duncan Phyfe benches with reeded edges and rolled arms, made about 1810 for a New York family.

The neoclassical marble mantel on the east wall is one of a pair ordered by Monroe in 1817 and installed in the State Dining Room. During the Roosevelt renovation of 1902 this one was moved to the Green Room and the other to the Red Room. A French bronze-doré clock made by Robert Robin (1742-1799), clockmaker to Louis XV and Louis XVI, sits on the mantel. Above the mantel hangs a portrait of Benjamin Franklin by Scottish artist David Martin. It was painted from life in London in 1767.

On each side of the fireplace are two almost identical and exceedingly rare mahogany work tables ingeniously designed with hidden compartments. Attributed to the New York workshop of Duncan Phyfe, they were probably made about 1810. A pair of Sheffield Argand lamps with oval-back mirrors, made in England in the early 19th century, stands on the work tables.

The carved and reeded mahogany pole-screen to the left of the fireplace is a fine example of the New York Regency style from the Federal period. The elliptical embroidered silk screen features the symbolic figure of Hope surrounded by a floral border.

Of particular note is a Sheraton armchair to the right of the mantel. Attributed to Phyfe's workshop, it is signed "Stephen van Rensselaer —Albany—Stuffed by L. Ackerman, New York." Acquired in 1971, it is

now upholstered in coral cut velvet. The wing chair to the left of the mantel dates from about 1810.

Doors on either side of the fireplace open to the East Room. Above the left door is an 1858 portrait of James K. Polk, one in the series of Presidential portraits painted by George P. A. Healy. Above the right door is a portrait of Benjamin Harrison, which was painted in 1895 by Eastman Johnson.

On the north wall, opposite the windows, are portraits by Gilbert Stuart of John Quincy Adams, painted in 1818, and his wife, Louisa. The paintings remained in the Adams family until a great-great-grandson, also named John Quincy Adams, presented them to the White House in 1970 and 1971. American paintings of later periods are also displayed on the north wall.

Below the portrait of Mrs. Adams hangs "Farmyard in Winter," which was painted by George H. Durrie in 1858 but shows a Connecticut farm of about 1825; below the portrait of President Adams is "The Mosquito Net," painted about 1908 by John Singer Sargent. Above the door leading to the Cross Hall is "Niagara Falls," a painting completed about 1851 by the Hudson River School artist John Frederick Kensett.

Identical mahogany pedestal pier tables of exceptional quality, made about 1815 in the workshop of Duncan Phyfe, stand beneath the paintings on the north wall. The cloverleaf tops are carved from King of Prussia marble quarried near Philadelphia. Possibly made as a pair, they were given to the White House in 1971 by different donors.

On the west wall hangs "Indian Guides," painted in 1849 by Alvan Fisher, another member of the Hudson River School. Below it hangs an

In 1816 Secretary of State James Monroe commissioned John Vanderlyn to paint a portrait of President James Madison (above left). When he succeeded Madison as President, Monroe was painted by Samuel F. B. Morse, best known as inventor of the telegraph but also a successful portrait artist. The likeness of Monroe (above) is assumed to be the one that was painted by Morse in the White House and completed in December 1819.

historically important 19th-century American cityscape, "Philadelphia in 1858," by Ferdinand Richardt. The painting was found in India, restored, and given to the White House in 1963. On each side of this painting are matching mahogany-and-gilt mirrored wall sconces dating from about 1800. The superb design and quality of the carving suggest the hand of Samuel McIntire, a noted craftsman working in Salem, Massachusetts.

Below these paintings is a handsome Duncan Phyfe settee of about 1810 that bears trademarks of his work—the tied reeds and clustered wheatears carved on the crest rail, the outcurved arms, and the reeded legs and seat rail. "Cluster-columned" drop-leaf library tables on either side of the settee are also attributed to Phyfe's workshop.

In front of the settee is a New York sofa table with unusual cloverleaf drop ends. The two Sheraton mahogany side chairs near it, probably made in New York about 1810, are rare for the period because of the upholstered backs, which indicate that they were originally intended for use in a drawing room. (Typical Sheraton open-back chairs could also be used in a dining room.)

On the sofa table are several historic pieces of Presidential silver, the most important being a Sheffield coffee urn of about 1785 that belonged to John Adams. Given to the White House in 1964, it was considered by President Adams to be among his "most prized possessions." An engraved, ribbon-hung ellipse above the spigot bears the initials "JAA" —John and Abigail Adams.

The two matching French candlesticks flanking the urn were bought by James Madison from James Monroe in 1803 and appear in subsequent inventories of the Madisons' household furnishings. Portraits of these two Presidents hang over the doors on the west wall: Madison, by the American artist John Vanderlyn; and Monroe, attributed to Samuel F. B. Morse.

"Lighter Relieving a Steamboat Aground," painted by George Caleb Bingham in 1846-47, hangs above the secretary in the Green Room. This genre scene portrays flatboatmen along the Mississippi or the Missouri River. Paintings on the west wall (right) depict both wilderness and city scenes of America in the mid-19th century: Alvan Fisher's 1849 "Indian Guides" and, below it, "Philadelphia in 1858" by Ferdinand Richardt.

THE BLUE ROOM

The oval Blue Room was completely redecorated in 1972 with many furnishings in the French Empire style—the decor chosen for the room by President James Monroe in 1817. A settee and seven of the original gilded chairs fashioned for Monroe by Parisian cabinetmaker Pierre-Antoine Bellangé form the nucleus of the present furnishings. The Empire style originated in France during Napoleon's reign and is characterized by richly carved rectilinear furniture based on Greek, Roman, and Egyptian forms. Typical decorative motifs evident in the Blue Room include acanthus foliage, imperial eagles, wreaths, urns, stars, and classical figures. Swags and brass mountings were often used in drapery designs.

The "elliptic saloon," with the oval rooms above and below it, formed the most elegant architectural feature of Hoban's plans for the White House. For the south wall of the Blue Room he designed French doors flanked by long windows. An oval portico with curving stairs was included in these original plans but was not built until 1824.

The Blue Room has always been used as a reception room except for a brief period during the administration of John Adams when it served as a south entrance hall. During the Madison Administration, architect Benjamin Latrobe designed a suite of classical-revival furniture for the room, but only some working drawings remain (see pages 112-13); the furnishings were destroyed in the fire of 1814.

When President Monroe redecorated the "large oval room" after the fire, he used the French Empire style. Monroe ordered a suite of French mahogany furniture through the American firm Russell and La Farge, with offices in Le Havre, France. However, the firm shipped gilded furniture instead, asserting that "mahogany is not generally admitted in the furniture of a Saloon, even at private gentlemen's houses." The order included a pier table; two large canapés, or sofas; 18 armchairs; two bergères, or armchairs with enclosed and upholstered sides, for the President and First Lady; 18 side chairs; four upholstered stools; and six footstools. Monroe's purchases for the Blue Room also included two large looking glasses; two screens; a bronze-doré clock; curtains that hung from arched gilt poles with eagles in the center; crimson flocked wallpaper; various lighting devices; ornaments in glass, porcelain, and bronze-doré; and an oval Aubusson rug, woven especially for this room and described in the bill of sale as green velvet with the national arms in the center. The furniture was decorated with carved sprigs of olive, although Monroe had asked for eagles. The upholstery was listed as double-warp satin in delicate crimson and two shades of gold, with an American eagle woven into the center of a wreath of laurel, the classical symbol of victory.

The bill from Russell and La Farge described these and other articles as "for the Account and Risk" of the President. In fact, Monroe ran some political risk, since there was considerable public pressure to buy only those goods made in the United States. William Lee, who was in charge of ordering the furniture, wrote somewhat defensively: "It must be acknowledged that the [French] articles are of the very first quality. . . ." Lee praised Bellangé's suite as "substantial heavy furniture, which should always remain in its place, and form, as it were, a part of the house; such as could be handed down through a succession of Presidents, suited to the dignity and character of the nation."

The Hannibal clock displayed on the mantel was the work of Denière and Matelin, noted French bronze casters who made many of the bronze-doré objects purchased in 1817 by President Monroe.

In 1837, President Van Buren redecorated the oval salon and started the tradition of a "blue room." In 1860, however, President Buchanan sold the Bellangé chairs and sofas at auction and replaced them with a Victorian rococo-revival suite (see pages 126-27); it served into the Theodore Roosevelt Administration. Certain of Monroe's other purchases were retained, including the Bellangé pier table, a French clock, and some of the ornaments. In the renovation of 1902, McKim, Mead & White restored the Empire decor and designed a set of furniture for the Blue Room based on the Bellangé originals. The walls were covered with a heavy ribbed steel-blue silk, woven to match a sample from the Napoleonic era. The new oak floor of herringbone parquet was uncarpeted.

Blue fabrics served as both wall coverings and draperies from 1902 until 1962, when the room was redecorated and the walls covered with cream-colored striped satin. By that time, the White House had been given three of the original Bellangé chairs, from which additional copies were made. A fourth chair was acquired in 1963.

In 1972 the room was completely redecorated again. Other Empire furnishings, including three more of the original Bellangé chairs, were added. The walls were covered in an American silk-screen reproduction of a French Directoire paper made about 1800, with friezes around the top and the bottom. The draperies, copied from an early 19th-century French design, are blue satin with handmade fringe and gold satin valances. The pattern of the upholstery is based on the original Monroe fabric, as recorded in John Vanderlyn's portrait of James Monroe (see page 116). One of the original Bellangé settees, acquired in 1978, was restored and placed here in 1981.

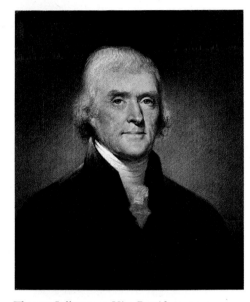

Thomas Jefferson as Vice President: an 1800 life portrait by Rembrandt Peale that was popularized by engravings.

The early 19th-century French Empire gilt wood chandelier is encircled by acanthus leaves. This motif is also carried out in the wallpaper frieze, the cornice, and the oval plaster ceiling medallion above the chandelier.

The French torchéres in front of the windows, made about 1810 and given to the White House in 1962, are in the form of classical female figures holding candelabra. Two matching 19th-century Louis XVI gilded console tables with marble tops stand between the windows. To the left of the center window hangs an 1819 portrait by John Wesley Jarvis of Andrew Jackson in uniform. To the right is a portrait of Thomas Jefferson by Rembrandt Peale, painted in Philadelphia in 1800, when Jefferson was Vice President. Jefferson was pleased with the painting, from which two engravings were made.

Other paintings in the Blue Room include a portrait of John Adams (on the west wall to the right of the windows) that was painted by John Trumbull about 1793, when Adams was Vice President. This is the first portrait of John Adams painted from life to be acquired for the White House; it was added to the room in 1986. Also hanging on the west wall is an 1859 portrait of John Tyler by George P. A. Healy; it is considered to be the finest of the series of Presidential portraits Healy painted for the White House under a commission from Congress. Among the documents illustrated in the portrait is one pertaining to Texas, which, although annexed on March 3, 1845, was not admitted to the Union until December—nine months after Tyler left office.

THE
BLUE
ROOM

One of Rembrandt Peale's many oval "porthole" portraits of George Washington hangs above the doorway to the Cross Hall. Flanking the doorway are two maritime scenes by Fitz Hugh Lane: "A View of Boston Harbor," painted in 1854, on the left, and "Baltimore Harbor," painted in 1850, on the right.

The early 19th-century marble mantel on the east wall, acquired in 1972, is in the neoclassical style and is similar to the two mantels purchased by Monroe from England. Above it is a New York Federal looking glass surmounted by a spread-wing American eagle. The precedent for such overmantel looking glasses in the Blue Room was set during the term of James Madison. One of the two Empire clocks purchased by Monroe is displayed on the mantel. Called the Hannibal clock, it bears a standing figure of the famous general from Carthage who led his troops, with some 40 elephants, across the Alps to fight the Romans in 218 B.C. The bronze-doré wall sconces hanging on either side of the looking glass were made in France about 1810. Winged creatures such as the griffins that support the candle arms were frequently used as decorative motifs on Empire furniture.

*This Bellangé bergère—
an armchair with closed and
upholstered sides—was purchased
in 1817 by James Monroe.*

To the right of the mantel hangs a portrait of Mrs. James Monroe still owned by the Monroe family. Painted by an unknown artist, possibly while her husband was United States Minister to France, it is one of two known life portraits of Mrs. Monroe. To the left of the mantel is a 20th-century copy of a Gilbert Stuart portrait of President Monroe; the original was one in a series of portraits of the first five Presidents painted by Stuart between 1818 and 1820. Stuart copied the head of Monroe from a life portrait he had painted in 1817.

Under the Monroe portrait is one of a pair of fine English console tables made between 1785 and 1790. The tables are most likely the work of a French craftsman living in England, which could explain the French influence in the details. Another pair of console tables is displayed under the Fitz Hugh Lane paintings. These Louis XVI half-moon tables with marble tops are attributed to Georges Jacob, a French cabinetmaker of the late 18th century. The mahogany marble-top table in the middle of the room has been in the White House since 1817, when it was purchased by President Monroe.

Two French porcelain vases in the room, made in Sèvres about 1800, were originally purchased by Monroe for the "Card Room"—now the Green Room. The vases are decorated with painted scenes of Passy, the Paris suburb where Benjamin Franklin lived when he was Minister to France.

Above a white Carrara marble mantel in the Blue Room, a double-paned Federal looking glass surmounted by an American eagle reflects the French Empire carved and gilded wood chandelier. The oval rug, woven in Peking around 1850, displays an Oriental adaptation of a French style.

THE RED ROOM

Furnished in the Empire style of 1810-30, the Red Room—one of the four state reception rooms in the White House—contains several pieces of furniture from the New York workshop of the French-born cabinetmaker Charles-Honoré Lannuier. An 1842 portrait by Henry Inman of Angelica Singleton Van Buren, President Martin Van Buren's daughter-in-law and official hostess, hangs above the mantel. A white marble bust of Van Buren in the neoclassical style appears in the portrait; it is one of three busts of Van Buren executed by Hiram Powers, for whom the President posed in 1836. One of these busts is displayed on the wall between the windows.

Benjamin Latrobe's 1803 drawing of the State Floor indicates that the Red Room served as "the President's Antichamber" for the Cabinet Room or President's Library next door. During the Madison Administration the antechamber became the "Yellow Drawing Room" and the scene of Dolley Madison's fashionable Wednesday night receptions. In "that centre of attraction," said a lady who knew her well, one saw "all these whom fashion, fame, beauty, wealth or talents, have render'd celebrated." The room has usually served as a parlor or sitting room; recent Presidents have held small dinner parties here.

In 1971 the Red Room was redecorated, preserving the American Empire style chosen in 1962 during the John F. Kennedy Administration. The elegance of the Red Room furniture derives from a combination of richly carved and finished woods with ormolu mounts (decorative hardware made of gilded bronze) in characteristic designs such as dolphins, acanthus leaves, lions' heads, and sphinxes. The furniture displays many motifs similar to those of the French pieces now in the Blue Room. Egyptian motifs were extensively used in French Empire furnishings following Napoleon's 1798-99 campaign in Egypt, and many of these same designs were adopted by cabinetmakers working in New York, Boston, and Philadelphia.

The furniture in the Red Room dates from the years 1810-30. The rare mahogany secretary-bookcase between the windows is attributed to Charles-Honoré Lannuier and exhibits the characteristic Empire rectilinear shape and ornamental brass hardware. The lancet arches in its glazed doors are a Gothic motif. Also attributed to Lannuier is the mahogany sofa table to the left of the fireplace. It has gilt winged-caryatid supports and the paw feet commonly used in Empire furniture. Lannuier's labeled masterpiece, and the most important piece of American Empire furniture in the White House Collection, is the marble-top gueridon, or small round table, opposite the fireplace. This table is made of mahogany and various fruitwoods with a trompe-l'oeil top of marble inlaid in a geometric pattern. Bronze-doré female heads surmount the delicately carved and reeded legs.

To the right of the fireplace is a graceful American Empire sofa with gilded dolphin feet. The sofa has the distinctive Empire curved back rail and scrolled arms. Behind it is a New York Empire card table, one of three tables in the room with a carved lyre design. An ancient stringed musical instrument, the lyre was widely used in Empire furniture as a decorative motif for table supports and chair backs.

The bronze-doré clock on the mantel, made by the well-known Parisian bronze caster Pierre Joseph Gouthière, was given to the White House in 1952 by President Vincent Auriol of France. The clock was designed during the late 18th century to play pastoral music on a miniature organ inside the gilded case.

The early 19th-century French gilt porcelain vases on either side of the clock are decorated with likenesses of George Washington and the Marquis de Lafayette. To the right of the fireplace is an American

Empire music stand holding sheet music for a march entitled "President Jackson's Grand March."

During the 19th century the Red Room was often used as a music room where families gathered on Sunday evenings. The furnishings occasionally included a piano or other musical instruments, such as the pianoforte and guitar ordered by Dolley Madison.

All the fabrics now in the Red Room were woven in the United States from French Empire designs. The walls are covered by a red twill satin fabric with a gold scroll design in the border. The furniture is upholstered in a damask of the same shade of red. An early 19th-century design inspired the draperies made of gold satin with red damask valances and handmade gold-and-red fringe. The beige, red, and gold rug is a reproduction of an early 19th-century French Savonnerie rug in the White House Collection; it was made for the room in 1965. The white marble mantel with caryatid figures is one of a pair ordered by Monroe that was originally placed in the State Dining Room. The French Empire chandelier was fashioned from carved and gilded wood about 1805. Carved eagles decorate the sconces on the east wall. Below them is a pair of French lamps of classical design.

This portrait of John James Audubon, exhibited on the west wall, was painted in Edinburgh in 1826 by Scottish artist John Syme. At the time, Audubon was in the British Isles seeking a publisher for his paintings of birds.

Descriptions in contemporary accounts and bills of sale indicate that Monroe purchased furnishings for the Red Room, as well as for the present-day Blue Room, in the prevailing Empire style. This style suited Monroe's desire to furnish the house in a manner that he considered appropriate to the dignity of the nation.

The room was called the Washington Parlor during the Polk and Tyler Administrations, when it contained Gilbert Stuart's portrait of George Washington. President and Mrs. Lincoln used the Red Room frequently for informal entertaining, and a contemporary reporter noted that the furniture was "very rich—of crimson satin and gold damask, with heavy gilded cornices to the windows and a profusion of ormolu work, vases, etc., some of which is very ancient, being bought or presented during Monroe's and Madison's Administrations."

Photographs taken during the latter half of the 19th century indicate that Victorian furnishings had been introduced to the Red Room (see page 130). During the renovation of 1902, many of these furnishings were removed and the collection of First Lady portraits, which had hung there toward the end of the 19th century, was transferred to the Ground Floor Corridor at the request of Edith Kermit Carow Roosevelt.

THE RED ROOM

The portrait of Dolley Madison (above), painted by Gilbert Stuart in 1804, was owned by the Madison family throughout her lifetime. An Empire sofa of about 1825 behind the round marble-top gueridon is flanked by a pair of early 19th-century New York mahogany card tables. On the wall hang two gilt wood eagle sconces made in England in the late 18th century. A still life by Severin Roesen, painted in 1850, hangs below Dolley Madison's portrait on the north wall. Displayed under the Roesen painting is one of a pair of rosewood Boston lyre tables with ormolu mounts (above), made about 1815. Two lamps in the room have porcelain bases made in Paris in the early 19th century by Philip-Louis Dagoty. The French Empire 36-light chandelier was made of carved and gilded wood about 1805. Above the sofa hang Albert Bierstadt's "View of the Rocky Mountains," signed and dated 1870, and a portrait of Col. William Drayton, painted by Samuel F. B. Morse in 1818.

THE STATE DINING ROOM

The State Dining Room, which now seats as many as 140 guests, was originally much smaller and served at various times as a drawing room, office, and Cabinet Room. Not until the administration of Andrew Jackson was it called the "State Dining Room," although it had been used for formal dinners by previous Presidents.

As the nation grew, so did the invitation list to official functions at the White House. In 1856 a reporter remarked that the State Dining Room was "not large enough, being 30 feet by 25 . . . as the Executive entertains Congress, the Supreme Court, diplomats and most of the distinguished people who visit Washington at his table, he requires a commodious and convenient dining-room." Toward the end of the 19th century, large dinners had to be held in the Cross Hall or in the East Room.

Such inconvenient makeshifts became unnecessary after the renovation of 1902 when architects McKim, Mead & White removed the main stairway from the west end of the Cross Hall and enlarged the State Dining Room to its present dimensions. The two Italian-marble mantels installed by Monroe were moved to the Red and Green Rooms; a single larger fireplace was constructed in the west wall. The architecture of the room was modeled on that of neoclassical English houses of the late 18th century. Below a new ceiling and a cornice of white plaster, natural oak wall paneling with Corinthian pilasters and a delicately carved frieze was installed. Three console tables with eagle supports, made by the A. H. Davenport Co. of Boston, were placed against the walls, and a silver chandelier and silver wall sconces were also added.

The dining room, when furnished, strongly reflected President Theodore Roosevelt's enthusiasm for big-game hunting. At his request, bison heads were carved on the new stone mantel, a large moose head was hung above the fireplace, and other big-game trophies were placed on the walls (see page 142). Two ornate 17th-century Flemish tapestries —one bearing lines from Virgil's eighth *Eclogue*—also decorated the wood-paneled room, along with draperies of rich green velvet. An architectural historian hailed the new dining room as "a stately hall of the Early English Renaissance." A critic, in the *Architectural Record* of April 1903, approvingly wrote that a White House "all carried out in strict Colonial would be but a monotonous and insipid mansion."

The 1902 classical woodwork was preserved in the Truman renovation of 1948-52 and was painted for the first time—a soft celadon green. Roosevelt's big-game trophies had long since been removed from the dining room. (The heads were sent to the Smithsonian Institution in 1923. Mrs. Theodore Roosevelt retrieved five of them in 1934 and six are

The mahogany dining table, surrounded by Queen Anne-style chairs, displays part of Monroe's gilt service purchased from France in 1817. The ornamental bronze-doré pieces are used today as table decorations for state dinners. The plateau centerpiece, with seven mirrored sections, measures 13 feet 6 inches in length when fully extended. Standing bacchantes holding crowns for candles or tiny bowls border the plateau. Three fruit baskets, supported by female figures, are filled with flowers. The two rococo-revival candelabra date from the Hayes Administration. The soft green and brown rug, specially woven in 1973 for this large room, reproduces a 17th-century Persian design.

THE STATE DINING ROOM

The State Dining Room sparkles in gold and white as the red-bordered Reagan china service makes its debut at a formal dinner for 118 guests on February 3, 1982. Vermeil bowls filled with white spring flowers adorn tables covered in white damask cloths and set with vermeil flatware. Above the mantel hangs George P. A. Healy's contemplative portrait of Abraham Lincoln (right), painted in 1869 and later acquired by the President's son Robert Todd Lincoln. Robert's widow bequeathed the portrait to the White House in 1939.

still there.) During the Truman renovation the original marble mantel with bison heads was replaced by a simple, black marble mantel. A reproduction of the bison-head mantel was installed in the State Dining Room in 1962.

At that time the wood paneling was painted antique ivory, and the sconces and chandelier were gilded. In 1981 the Queen Anne-style chairs, chosen for the room in 1902, were reupholstered in a gold horsehair material, a durable fabric popular in the 19th century. Silk-damask draperies of a golden hue and delicately curved valances were placed at the windows the same year.

Carved into the mantel below George P. A. Healy's portrait of President Lincoln is an inscription from a letter written by John Adams on his second night in the White House: "I Pray Heaven to Bestow the Best of Blessings on THIS HOUSE and on All that shall hereafter Inhabit it. May none but Honest and Wise Men ever rule under this Roof."

THE FAMILY DINING ROOM

The room at the northwest corner of the State Floor, now known as the Family Dining Room, served as the "Public Dining Room" in the early 1800's. It was one of two dining rooms separated by a staircase in James Hoban's original plan (see page 110). President James Monroe held state dinners here, while the other room served as his Cabinet Room.

In the late afternoon, Monroe and his guests gathered in the oval salon—now the Blue Room—before proceeding to the dining room, where the newly purchased French gilt service and vermeil flatware provided an elegant table setting. The guests were seated according to a carefully arranged plan, and Monroe's personal household servants passed the dishes in the formal French manner. When the ladies withdrew after dessert, the gentlemen lingered for a few glasses of wine— Monroe liked to replace the traditional Madeira with a native wine made from scuppernong grapes. Although Americans found the new vermeil service sumptuous, many European dignitaries, expecting more from a chief of state, thought it merely well suited to a private citizen of some means.

The furnishings in the dining room in President Monroe's time were collected by William Lee, a Treasury official and friend of Monroe's, who was his purchasing agent for the refurnishing of the White House following its rebuilding after the fire of 1814. The furniture included two pier tables used by the Madisons in their official residences while the White House was being rebuilt and two sideboards, which the Monroes sold to the White House from their personal furnishings. A local craftsman, William Worthington, made a large sideboard for the room, plus a dining table and 16 new chairs. The chairs were all upholstered in glossy black horsehair. Light was provided by four lion's-head sconces, a gilded lamp decorated with swans, and a pair of antique green bronze lamps with stars and swans.

There is little information about the color scheme in the dining room during Monroe's Presidency or, in fact, for much of the 19th century until the Victorian period. The rich Victorian splendor was recorded in contemporary photographs and was finally supplanted in 1902 by a classical-revival style.

Part of President Monroe's 1817 purchases for the White House consisted of a large order from the French silversmith Jacques-Henri Fauconnier (1776-1839). This order included two silver tureens with platters and liners, ladles, a large number of fluted silver plates, serving pieces, and 36 place settings of vermeil flatware. Reproductions of the vermeil flatware, as well as the surviving original pieces, are used for state dinners today.

The mirrored plateau centerpiece on the table in the Family Dining Room is called "Hiawatha's Boat." Inspired by a poem by Henry Wadsworth Longfellow, its design motifs include a canoe with its sail set and a figure of the Indian Hiawatha in its stern. Mrs. Ulysses S. Grant chose the plateau for the White House. A portrait of Brig. Gen. John Hartwell Cocke, mounted on his horse Roebuck, hangs above the fireplace.

A Hepplewhite linen press (above left) is now used for storing silver trays; the coffee urn and tray displayed on the chest are part of the everyday White House silver. A Philadelphia library bookcase of 1800 (center) displays porcelain from the Benjamin Harrison Administration. An original brass pull (top right) from a Sheraton sideboard commemorates George Washington, whose profile is shown in relief. Pieces from early 19th-century flatware services include a vermeil-handled fruit knife, three serving spoons, and a pearl-handled fruit knife.

Eventually, public functions were held in the present State Dining Room, and the Family Dining Room was kept for the private use of the President's family. By the Jackson Administration the size of this room had been reduced by the creation of a butler's pantry at the west end, eliminating an original fireplace and two windows. The architectural details of the room today date from the 1902 renovation, when the vaulted ceiling and cornice with its classical frieze were installed. In 1961, another dining room on the second floor was provided for the family of the President. The Family Dining Room is currently used for official occasions involving a small number of guests.

The painted yellow walls are accented by white woodwork and a white ceiling. Above the cornice is a plaster decoration featuring an eagle. The Louis XVI mantel, acquired in 1962, was made in France in the 1770's. A white eagle appears in decorative relief against its dark greenish marble. The gilded clock on the mantel is typical of French clocks made for the American trade during the first quarter of the 19th century. Made by Dubuc of Paris, it is decorated with an American eagle and a standing figure of George Washington.

Above the mantel hangs a portrait of Brig. Gen. John Hartwell Cocke of Bremo, Virginia. It was painted in 1859 by Edward Troye, an American artist noted for his paintings of race horses. General Cocke, in military uniform, is shown at the time of the War of 1812, mounted on his horse Roebuck.

The furniture in the room is from the Federal period. The Sheraton-style mahogany dining table, with finely reeded saber legs, was made in Maryland about 1800. The silver-mirrored centerpiece was made in 1872 by the Gorham Manufacturing Company of Rhode Island and selected for the White House by Mrs. Ulysses S. Grant. The New York Sheraton chairs are identical in style to those used in the President's Dining Room on the second floor.

The most important piece of furniture in the room is an early Federal library bookcase, one of a pair built in Philadelphia about 1800. It is made of mahogany with inlaid satinwood bands and quarter fans. This bookcase and its mate in the Mabel Brady Garvan Collection at the Yale University Art Gallery are the only pair of Federal-period American bookcases known to exist.

A New England Federal sideboard of the early 1800's stands along the west wall and has a drapery-effect carving on the sliding door of the tambour section. A Hepplewhite-style mahogany linen press has been modified to provide storage space for silver trays. The linen press, with delicate inlay work, was made in Annapolis about 1790 and once belonged to the family of William Paca, a signer of the Declaration of Independence and later a governor of Maryland.

On the west wall hangs a 1902 portrait of Edith Roosevelt by Theobald Chartran, with the White House South Portico appearing in the background. Also in the room are several 19th-century American landscapes and genre scenes, including William Ranney's "Boys Crabbing."

THE EAST SITTING HALL

"All sorts of people come upon all sorts of errands," wrote one of Abraham Lincoln's secretaries, describing the crowds of people who filled the second-floor hall while waiting to see the President. " 'Is Old Abe in?' 'If you mean the President of the United States, this is Congress day. Are you a member of the Senate or of the House? The messenger will take in any member's card.' " Until 1902, when the President's offices were moved to the newly constructed West Wing, dignitaries, inventors, and politicians and their constituents waited in this hall for an opportunity to see the Chief Executive.

Hoban's original Palladian-style window with fanlight panes dominates the sitting room. Many of the architectural details date from 1952, including the acanthus-leaf-and-bracket cornice, the outer window frame with 13 stars, and the inner frame with circular medallions. The lemon-yellow draperies of silk-and-cotton taffeta were hung in 1981. Lighting fixtures include an English cut-glass chandelier of the Georgian period and a pair of hexagonal Chinese vases made into lamps.

The furniture in the room includes a mahogany lolling armchair, also called a Martha Washington chair, to the right of a small Chippendale-style tilt-top piecrust table. To the left are a mahogany wing chair, made about 1795 in Massachusetts, and an American card table, from about 1820. The small tambour desk by the north wall is attributed to English-born craftsmen John and Thomas Seymour, a father and son who opened shop in Boston in 1794. Two sewing tables, possibly made by the Seymours as well, flank the upholstered Sheraton-style sofa. On either side of the early 19th-century sofa table is a Louis XVI painted armchair, made in the late 18th century. One of those chairs was used by George Washington in the President's House in Philadelphia. To the right of the window stands a New England Hepplewhite chest of drawers, from about 1790, which is ornamented with such classical inlays as fans, urns, and bellflowers.

Above the tambour desk hangs "Florida Sunrise," painted by Martin Johnson Heade (1819-1904) late in his life, after he had taken up residence in St. Augustine, Florida. The first scene of the southern United States acquired for the White House, this landscape shows the American Luminists' combination of precise drawing and the study of light.

To the left of the door on the north wall hang "Mouth of the Delaware," painted by Thomas Birch in 1828, and, below it, "The Pavilion, Gloucester, Mass.," a 1918 scene by William J. Glackens that reflects the influence of French Impressionists on American artists in the early 20th century. Also displayed in this room is an 1876 autumn landscape painted by the Hudson River School artist Jasper Cropsey.

The East Sitting Hall, overlooking the Treasury Building, serves as an informal sitting room for the adjacent Queens' Suite and Lincoln Suite. During most of the 19th century, the east end of the second floor was devoted to official business. When the President's offices were moved to the West Wing in 1902, this area became part of the White House family quarters. It is now used by personal, rather than official, guests of the President's family.

*This small mahogany tambour desk,
attributed to John and Thomas Seymour
of Boston, dates from about 1800.
A curly-maple veneer band, a characteristic
of the Seymour style, edges the hinged top,
which folds out to form a writing board.
This desk is one of only three the Seymours
made in a pediment design.*

THE QUEENS' BEDROOM

The Queens' Suite, consisting of a small sitting room and a bedroom—called the Rose Guest Room until the mid-1960's—has formed part of the White House family quarters since the Roosevelt renovation of 1902. Previously, these rooms were used by the President's staff. The bedroom was occupied by President Lincoln's private secretaries, John Hay and John G. Nicolay. The sitting room served as Hay's office and years later as an emergency telegraph room while President Garfield struggled to recover from an assassin's bullet.

During the 20th century, the Queens' Suite, sharing the East Sitting Hall with the Lincoln Suite, has been used by a number of distinguished guests, including Queen Elizabeth of Great Britain (now the Queen Mother); Queen Wilhelmina and Queen Juliana of the Netherlands; Queen Frederika of Greece; Princess Elizabeth of Great Britain, who returned a few years later as Queen Elizabeth II; and most recently by Princess Anne, who visited the White House with her brother Prince Charles in 1970. Both Winston Churchill and V. M. Molotov, Soviet Minister for Foreign Affairs, occupied the Queens' Suite at different times while conferring with President Franklin D. Roosevelt during World War II.

The Queens' Bedroom, which overlooks Lafayette Park to the north of the White House, is comfortably furnished in the styles of the American Federal period. The furniture includes a tambour secretary placed between the windows, the work of the Boston cabinetmakers John and Thomas Seymour. Made of mahogany, the desk is inlaid with satinwood and curly maple. The two inlaid card tables on either side of the four-poster bed are also attributed to the Seymours. The bed is thought to have belonged to Andrew Jackson. The carved Federal sofa displays the fine craftsmanship of Samuel McIntire of Salem, Massachusetts, in its gracefully scrolled arms and the floral decorations of the top rail. Complementing the rose-and-white scheme is a Hereke rug from the mid-19th century, acquired in 1971. The cut-glass chandelier was made in England in the late 18th century.

The carved wooden mantel on the west wall was formerly in Burnside, a Philadelphia house built in 1792. Above the mantel is a late 17th-century trumeau, a mirror and flower painting framed together. This striking piece was presented to the White House in 1951 by Princess Elizabeth on behalf of her father, King George VI. Also in the room are Thomas Sully's portrait of English actress Fanny Kemble (above the sofa), painted in 1834 when she was on a tour of the United States, and a portrait of Emily Donelson, Andrew Jackson's niece and hostess, painted by Ralph E. W. Earl in 1830.

The Queens' Bedroom, named for its many royal guests, is decorated in shades of rose and white. Most of the fabrics in the room are reproductions of period designs. The mantel is of carved wood in the classical style, with fluted pilasters on either side. The wing chair by the fireplace was made in Massachusetts about 1810. The work table beside it features a fabric bag suspended below to hold letters or sewing.

THE LINCOLN BEDROOM

Decorated primarily with American Victorian furnishings from 1850-70, the Lincoln Bedroom is used today as a guest room for friends of the President's family. The Victorian period takes its name from Victoria, Queen of England, and lasted from about 1840 until the end of the century. Several distinctive styles flourished during this period, all based on earlier styles and marked by exaggeration of form and ornamentation. The idea of installing bedroom furniture from the Lincoln era in this room—used by Lincoln as an office and Cabinet Room—was conceived by President Truman. The imposing rosewood bed, more than eight feet

long and almost six feet wide, is thought to have been part of a large
quantity of furniture purchased by Mrs. Lincoln in 1861. An 1862 news-
paper account indicates that the bed stood in a second-floor guest room;
although Abraham Lincoln probably never used the bed, several other
Presidents have, including Woodrow Wilson and Theodore Roosevelt.
Mrs. Roosevelt was fond of the marble-top rosewood table in the middle
of the room, which was probably designed to match the bed. The ornate
carving on both pieces of furniture, including fanciful birds, grapevines,
and flowers, is typical of the Victorian rococo-revival style.

Between 1830 and 1902 the room now known as the Lincoln Bedroom served Presidents as either an office or as a Cabinet Room. When all second-floor offices were moved to the West Wing during the Roosevelt renovation, this area became part of the private family quarters. The Lincoln Suite, which is now used for personal guests of the President's family and adjoins the East Sitting Hall, includes the bedroom and the Lincoln Sitting Room.

Many of the Victorian furnishings in the bedroom were placed there during the Truman Administration when the patterned Brussels carpet and the Lincoln bed were installed. The chandelier, acquired in 1972, resembles one depicted in an engraving of the room during Lincoln's term. The sofa and three matching chairs, given to the White House in 1954, are believed to have been used in the mansion during the Lincoln Administration. The two identical slipper chairs, also dating from the Lincoln period, are upholstered in antique yellow-and-green Morris velvet; one of the chairs was sold after the President's assassination but was returned to the White House as a gift in 1961.

The rocking chair near the window is a replica of the chair Lincoln sat in at Ford's Theatre the night of his assassination. Slender curves embellish the legs of the walnut Victorian table beside it. Round tables, their tops inset with dark marble, flank the bed and are from a set of three bought by President Jackson for the East Room; they were made by the Philadelphia cabinetmaker Anthony Quervelle.

The walnut bureau with full-length mirror has been in the White House for more than a century, although its exact origins are unknown. In a catalogue of White House furnishings, Mrs. Herbert Hoover noted that a previous resident described the piece affectionately as the "old bureau where I used to do my pompadour every morning." Its serpentine curved drawers and ornamental carving are typical Victorian forms.

A late-Empire marble-and-ormolu clock, 19 inches high, stands on the mantel in the Lincoln Bedroom. The clock was probably purchased during the Jackson Administration.

Along the west wall are four of Lincoln's Cabinet chairs, believed to have been purchased for the White House during the Polk Administration. To the left of the fireplace is a desk that Lincoln used at the "summer White House," a brick and stucco cottage on the extensive grounds of the Soldiers' Home—a few miles northeast of the Executive Mansion. The desk was transferred to the White House during the Hoover Administration.

Displayed on the desk is one of five holograph copies of the Gettysburg Address, delivered by President Lincoln on November 19, 1863. The speech dedicated the national cemetery at Gettysburg, Pennsylvania, where Gen. Robert E. Lee's army had been defeated the previous July. This copy, on three sheets of paper, was the second version prepared by Lincoln at the request of historian George Bancroft. The first was returned to Lincoln because it was unsuitable for reproduction by lithography. With it came a request for another, written only on one side of each sheet of paper. Lincoln sent both copies to Col. Alexander Bliss, Bancroft's stepson. The Colonel kept the second copy, since called the "Bliss copy." It is now in the White House. This version is the only one of the five that is signed, dated, and titled by Abraham Lincoln.

Lincoln especially liked the portrait of Andrew Jackson, which hangs to the left of the bed. The painting is attributed to Miner K. Kellogg. The portrait of Mary Todd Lincoln to the right of the bed was painted, from photographs, in 1925 by Katherine Helm, daughter of Mrs. Lincoln's half-sister, Emily Todd Helm. Widow of a Confederate general, Emily Helm visited the White House in 1863 with Katherine. The portrait, given to the White House by Mrs. Robert Todd Lincoln, shows a youthful Mary Lincoln in elegant finery.

Used by President Lincoln as his office, this room overlooked the unfinished Washington Monument and the nearby Virginia hills and was one of the few rooms to escape Mrs. Lincoln's extensive redecorating. An observer in 1862 noted that the room "is very neatly papered, but should be better furnished. All the furniture is exceedingly old, and is too ricketty to venerate." C. K. Stellwagen commented when he made a sketch of the room (see page 128) in 1864 that the wallpaper was "dark green with a gold star," the carpet "dark green with buff figure in diamonds," and the upholstery faded.

Lincoln and his son Tad: a miniature oil by Francis B. Carpenter, a White House guest in 1864.

Throughout the Civil War an inevitable mass of paperwork littered the office. Maps tracing the course of the war covered the walls; on the desk and tables were newspapers, stacks and bundles of papers, mail, and requests from office seekers. Two large wicker wastebaskets held the debris.

To the right of the mantel is an engraving of Francis B. Carpenter's 1864 painting "First Reading of the Emancipation Proclamation before Lincoln's Cabinet." The reading took place in this room on July 22, 1862; the picture shows how the room was furnished at that time. The proclamation, intended by Lincoln primarily as a war measure, declared freedom for all slaves in the regions then in rebellion. Lincoln's Secretary of State William Seward advised him that the proclamation should be delayed until after a military victory by Union forces to make it appear an act of national strength—not a despairing last resort.

The Battle of Antietam provided a Union victory, and on September 22 a preliminary proclamation was issued, to become effective when signed by the President in 100 days. In this room, following the traditional New Year's reception of January 1, 1863, President Lincoln signed the proclamation—and gave it the force of law.

A painting above the desk, acquired in 1972 and entitled "Watch Meeting—or Waiting for the Hour," depicts slaves and a few friends waiting on December 31, 1862, for midnight to bring their new days of freedom. This painting, by William T. Carlton, was given to President Lincoln and hung in the White House during the last years of his administration. On the north wall hangs a 20th-century portrait of Lincoln by Douglas Volk.

THE LINCOLN SITTING ROOM

The Lincoln Sitting Room is furnished in late-Empire and Victorian styles to harmonize with the decor of the adjoining Lincoln Bedroom. A small corner room, it served as a busy office for Presidential staff members during most of the 19th century.

The small room at the southeast corner of the second floor was apparently little used in the mansion's early years. As late as 1825, an inventory described it simply as "empty." However, English novelist Charles Dickens, in an account of his visit to the White House during the Tyler Administration, wrote that the room was then used as the President's office, although he was not favorably impressed with either its size or its furnishings. During the Polk Administration, it doubled as a bedroom and office for the President's nephew and private secretary, J. Knox Walker.

The room continued to be used as an office for various Presidential clerks and secretaries until 1902, when all offices were moved to the newly constructed West Wing. It then became part of the family quarters. The present decor of the sitting room, which complements the Victorian character of the adjoining Lincoln Bedroom, dates from the Reagan Administration. A red, brown, and beige cotton fabric covers the walls, window shades, and valances. The pattern of the floor-length curtains, derived from a paisley design, continues this color scheme.

The four rosewood chairs are part of a set purchased by Mrs. Lincoln for the White House. Their serpentine contours, cabriole front legs, and reverse-curve back legs are typical of some Victorian furniture. The development of a special laminating process enabled cabinetmakers to bend stylish wood veneers (usually rosewood or mahogany) in imaginative ways. These chairs are thought to date from about 1860. Cut-velvet upholstery fabrics, such as the one covering the chairs, were in vogue during the Victorian era.

The cut-and-frosted glass chandelier is probably American and also dates from about 1860. Diamond-pointed prisms circle its shaft and hang from its six candle arms. Similar prisms decorate a glass vase on the nest of Chinese red-lacquer tables. A plaster sculpture group designed about 1860 by American artist John Rogers, entitled "Neighboring Pews," stands in front of the south window. Genre sculptures of this type, mass-produced and sold inexpensively, were popular in the second half of the 19th century.

The small mahogany desk in the corner was made by James Hoban, the original architect of the White House. The French Empire clock on the desk dates from the period 1825-30.

In addition to numerous engravings and mementos of Lincoln's time, the sitting room contains early renderings of Pierre Charles L'Enfant's plan for the District of Columbia and 19th-century prints illustrating the growth of the city. (L'Enfant designed the "Federal District" at the invitation of President Washington.)

THE
TREATY
ROOM

The Treaty Room—the name chosen during the term of John F. Kennedy to reflect the many important decisions made there—served as the Cabinet Room for ten administrations, beginning with Andrew Johnson's in 1865. When all Presidential staff offices were moved to the West Wing in 1902, it became a sitting room. Since the early 1960's the room has been furnished to resemble the Cabinet Room during President Ulysses S. Grant's term of office. The Victorian furnishings include many pieces bought by Grant for the room as well as others of a similar style that have been used elsewhere in the White House since the late 19th century.

The Treaty Room normally serves as a private meeting room for the President. Since its restoration in 1961, it has also been used for the signing of several important documents. On October 7, 1963, President Kennedy signed the United States instrument of ratification of the Treaty for a Partial Nuclear Test Ban. On September 30, 1972, President Nixon signed the United States instrument of ratification of the Treaty on the Limitation of Anti-ballistic Missile Systems.

The furniture in the room dating from the Grant Administration includes the Cabinet table, several upholstered chairs, a bentwood swivel armchair, a sofa, and the marble-and-malachite clock on the writing table. The Treaty Room also contains a number of other historical White House pieces: an ornate gilded overmantel mirror from the Pierce Administration; a pair of bronze-doré standing candelabra given to Andrew Jackson at his inauguration in 1829 by a friend, Gen. Robert E. Patterson; and a small desk that once belonged to Julia Dent Grant. The round mahogany table in the corner is one of the set of three purchased by President Jackson for the East Room in 1829 and made by Anthony Quervelle, a Paris-born cabinetmaker who settled and worked in Philadelphia. (The other tables are in the Lincoln Bedroom.)

The cut-glass chandelier, purchased for the Treaty Room in 1978, perfectly complements the Victorian decor of the room. Made around 1850 by the Osler Company in Bristol, England, the electrified oil fixture has twenty arms in two tiers. Each arm is fitted with a glass oil font and a frosted-glass globe etched in the Greek key motif.

The deep wine-colored drapes and green flocked-velvet wallpaper are copies of typical Victorian designs. The geometric border of the wallpaper is based on the one in the room in the Peterson house—across the

Facsimiles of treaties signed by the United States hang in the Treaty Room, which is furnished in Victorian style. The documents represent the 10 administrations that used this as a Cabinet Room between 1865 and 1902.

street from Ford's Theatre—where Abraham Lincoln was taken after he was shot and where he died.

The magnificent walnut table and a set of "walnut French stuffed chairs" were ordered in 1869 from the New York firm Pottier and Stymus by President Grant for his Cabinet Room. During the renovation of 1902 the Cabinet chairs, a Victorian interpretation of Louis XVI furniture, were sold as souvenirs to Theodore Roosevelt's Cabinet members for a token $5 apiece. The massive Victorian table was made with eight locking drawers so that each Cabinet member could secure his papers between meetings. The table and original chairs appear in an 1899 painting, hanging to the right of the doorway, by Theobald Chartran and entitled "The Signing of the Peace Protocol," which took place in this room on August 12, 1898. The document, which established an armistice in the Spanish-American War, was signed by French Ambassador Jules Cambon on behalf of Spain. A three-handled silver cup made by Louis Tiffany, presented to Cambon on this occasion by President William McKinley, was acquired by the White House in 1972 and is now displayed in the room. On March 26, 1979, President Carter had the conference table moved to the north grounds for the signing of the Egyptian-Israeli peace treaty.

The Victorian heart-back chairs, now placed around the table and

THE
TREATY
ROOM

The marble-and-malachite clock, purchased by President Grant in 1869, includes barometer and calendar dials and a thermometer. Andirons belonging to Zachary Taylor, and believed to have been used in the White House during his Presidency, combine Chinese and rococo motifs. In George P. A. Healy's painting "The Peacemakers," President Lincoln confers with his military advisers Generals Sherman and Grant and Admiral Porter on board the River Queen, *anchored at City Point near Richmond, Virginia. The meeting was held on March 28, 1865, to discuss plans on how best to end the Civil War.*

upholstered in black horsehair, were previously used in the Family and State Dining Rooms and are believed to have been in the White House since the James K. Polk Administration. Hanging above the desk is a painting, attributed to Francis B. Carpenter, of the reception in the East Room given in 1864 for Gen. Ulysses S. Grant by President and Mrs. Lincoln, just before Grant's appointment as head of the Union armies (see pages 122-23).

One of a pair of Philadelphia astral lamps from the Victorian period stands on the round table in the corner. Astral lamps were usually ornate and columnar in design with an Argand burner and a ring-shaped oil reservoir that also served as the rest for the glass shade. The lamps were designed so that the reservoir cast no shadow on the table. The side chairs near the window, upholstered in wine-red velvet, have miniature portraits of President Taylor and President Van Buren carved on the crest rails.

To the left of the window hangs a portrait of Zachary Taylor in uniform, painted about 1848 by Joseph H. Bush. The painting was presented to the White House by Taylor's daughter, Mrs. Betty Taylor Dandridge, sometime before 1890. Two other Presidential portraits hang in the Treaty Room: Ulysses S. Grant, painted by Henry Ulke in 1871, and Andrew Johnson, painted by Eliphalet F. Andrews in 1880.

THE
CENTER
HALL

The Center Hall, brightened by a yellow-and-white color scheme, serves as a spacious drawing room for the First Family and Presidential guests, including many foreign dignitaries, who are received in the Yellow Oval Room. When the eastern end of the second floor was used for Presidential offices, the Center Hall area, then known as the "Great Passage," contained a partition to keep the public from wandering into the private quarters. President Arthur made the western end of the hall into a "picture gallery, promenade, and smoking room." During World War II, as playwright Robert Sherwood recalled, the long corridor was dark and dismal, cluttered by ships' models, prints, old photographs, and hundreds of books.

Recent First Families have used the hall to display paintings by American artists. At the west end of the Center Hall hangs Mary Cassatt's "Young Mother and Two Children," which reveals the influence of the French artists Manet and Degas. Also displayed is a painting on loan from the Hirshhorn Museum and Sculpture Garden, Smithsonian Institution, entitled "Nymph and Sea," by Childe Hassam, who adopted the technique and palette of the French Impressionists. Paintings by other American artists who followed the French Impressionists hang in the hall as well: "Bouquet with Ferns" by William J. Glackens, "Formal Gardens" by Colin Campbell Cooper, and "Evening at the Lock" by Theodore Robinson, which is on loan to the White House.

During the Truman renovation of 1948-52, the room was unified by the installation of a cornice and bookshelves. A pair of late 18th-century English chandeliers was also added. Furnishings acquired during the Kennedy Administration include the Sheraton settee and four matching chairs. The 12-panel Chinese coromandel screen along the south wall, which dates from the late 17th-century K'ang Hsi period, was given to the White House in 1964.

The octagonal pedestal writing desk, which divides the hall into two receiving rooms, was donated to the White House during the Kennedy Administration. This rare partners' desk dates from the late 18th century and is made in two halves that may be separated for use against a wall or combined in the center of a room. It was placed in the room again in 1981, when most of the second floor was refurbished.

Other pieces in the hall made in the late 18th or early 19th centuries include the New England sofa table in front of the shelves on the north wall, the pair of mahogany Chippendale looking glasses on either side of the entrance to the West Sitting Hall, and the two matching English Chippendale rococo torchères, or candlestands, that flank the door to the Yellow Oval Room.

Filled with furnishings from the 18th and 19th centuries, the Center Hall serves as an informal sitting room for the President's family and guests and as a reception area for the Yellow Oval Room, to the left.

The mahogany chair-back settee (below) and four matching chairs in the Center Hall are among the finest existing examples of Philadelphia craftsmanship in the Sheraton style. They date from the years 1800-10.

Among the Federal-period furniture in the Center Hall is a Sheraton card table, one of a matching pair attributed to John and Thomas Seymour of Boston. Made of mahogany and satinwood, the folding-top card tables were acquired during the Nixon Administration.

THE CENTER HALL

A 17th-century coromandel screen accents the south wall of the Center Hall, near the entrance to the Yellow Oval Room. The 12-panel lacquer screen separates into two parts; since the Reagan redecoration of 1981, it has been displayed as a single unit. The use of this type of lacquerware for screens and furniture began in the mid-17th century; they were produced mainly in the Henan province of China. Such screens made "in Chinese varnish" reached a peak of popularity in 18th-century Europe, especially at the court of Louis XIV. The black ground emphasizes the rich colors that have softened and darkened over time.

"Young Mother and Two Children" was painted by Mary Cassatt in 1908. Born in Pennsylvania, the artist spent most of her life in France; her work shows the influence of Manet and Degas. Children were a favorite subject, and she painted them with strength and without sentimentality.

THE YELLOW OVAL ROOM

On New Year's Day, 1801, President John Adams held the first White House reception in this oval room which, although incomplete, contained some handsome furnishings and was greatly admired. During Thomas Jefferson's term, this room was called the "Ladies' Drawing Room," and the President's married daughters, when visiting their father, entertained friends here. In 1809, Dolley Madison had the furniture upholstered in yellow damask and had curtains—with festoons and fringes—made of the same material. All the original furnishings were destroyed in the fire of 1814. After numerous changes in use and appearance, the oval drawing room was furnished in the Louis XVI style during the Kennedy Administration. The yellow color scheme chosen again at that time continues as the dominant theme still.

The neoclassical style of Louis XVI, King of France, was strongly influenced by furnishings discovered during the excavations at Pompeii and Herculaneum and at sites in Greece in the mid-18th century. Furniture designs were characterized by simple oval and rectilinear forms, and a lightness and delicacy of color and line that disappeared in the French Empire style that followed.

Architectural changes made in the room in 1974 included adding a chair rail and a plaster ceiling centerpiece. This oval ceiling medallion echoes the shape of the room; it bears the acanthus-leaf and swag motifs that were prominent in Louis XVI neoclassical designs. The furniture, too, reflects the period. It is distinguished by tapered, sometimes fluted, chair legs; delicately carved chair and sofa frames painted in pale colors; and square or oval chair backs.

The rare set of four carved and gilded armchairs was made by C. Sené, a well-known French craftsman of the Louis XVI period. The small writing table of the same period is stamped "Leleu," the name of another famous French cabinetmaker. Its top drawer contains a compartment with inkwell and sand holder. A painted settee and two armchairs, part of an American suite of a slightly later period, once belonged to President Monroe. They are decorated with scrollwork and female figures. The suite of Louis XVI furniture, made about 1800 by Jean-Baptiste Lelarge, includes four side chairs and two armchairs.

The Italian Carrara marble mantel, featuring female figures in high relief, is believed to have been carved by a European sculptor in the early 19th century. The gilded bronze clock on the mantel is the work of an 18th-century French clockmaker; the pistol-handled urns of Chinese porcelain date from the early 19th century.

The Yellow Oval Room, decorated in the Louis XVI style of late 18th-century France, serves as a formal drawing room for the President's family and as a reception room for foreign chiefs of state and heads of government before state luncheons and dinners. The colors of its furnishings reflect the name of the room: yellow silk draperies, installed in 1972; an antique Turkish Hereke rug, added in 1974; and two comfortable sofas, upholstered in yellow damask and placed here in 1981. Paintings by late 19th-century American artists displayed in the room include Jasper Cropsey's "Under the Palisades in October," which hangs above the mantel.

Two French commodes of the Louis XV style flank the mantel. They
are elaborately inlaid and supported by delicate cabriole legs. The candelabra that now stand on the commodes were a gift from the British
government, presented by Princess Elizabeth during her 1951 visit to
the United States. Intricately crafted from marble, bronze-doré, and
blue spar stone, they were made in England about 1770. The Empire-
style chandelier of bronze-doré and crystal was made in France about
1820. The two large vertical mirrors on the west wall, with Adam-style
carved and gilded frames, are English, dating from the late 18th century. Under the mirrors stand two carved and gilded console tables that
exhibit the fine craftsmanship of the Louis XVI era. They are half-moon
in shape and feature elaborate openwork carving along the apron. Formerly in the collection of the Chateau de Condé, they were acquired by
the White House in 1973. The rug is a 19th-century Turkish Hereke,
woven in a French design.

Noteworthy paintings by American artists hang in the Yellow Oval
Room. To the left of the door leading from the second-floor corridor is
"Shinnicock Hills, Long Island," an impressionist landscape painted by
William Merritt Chase in 1900. Albert Bierstadt's study of storm clouds,
from about 1880, hangs to the right of this door. On the west wall hangs
the 1877 painting "Castle Rock, Marblehead, Massachusetts," by Alfred
T. Bricher, known for his scenes of the Massachusetts coast. A city-
scape, "New York Harbor and the Battery," painted by Andrew Mel-
rose about 1887, is displayed on the east wall, along with "Cliffs of
Green River, Wyoming," a majestic and romantic view of the American
West by Thomas Moran. Jasper Cropsey's "Under the Palisades in October" hangs over the fireplace. This 1895 painting of the high cliffs

*"New York Harbor
and the Battery,"
by New Jersey
landscape artist
Andrew Melrose,
provides an
impressionistic
glimpse of the city
waterfront in
about 1887. In the
background stands
the Statue of Liberty,
which was unveiled
on October 28,
1886. This painting
was added to the
White House
Collection in 1973.*

**THE
YELLOW
OVAL
ROOM**

along the Hudson River illustrates the almost mystical reverence for wilderness that was characteristic of the Hudson River School, the first truly American school of artists.

According to an inventory of 1825, the Yellow Oval Room was used as a bedroom; it became a family room during the administration of Andrew Jackson. Mrs. Fillmore found a straw carpet left from President Taylor's occupancy that was described in a contemporary account as "made filthy by tobacco-chewers." She had a used Brussels carpet cleaned, sent for her piano and her daughter's harp, and made this the library when Congress appropriated $5,000 to purchase books for the White House; it remained a library through the 1920's. In 1889, according to an aide to President Benjamin Harrison, the first White House Christmas tree was displayed here.

Grover Cleveland, as well as Benjamin Harrison, used this room as an office. Franklin D. Roosevelt and Harry S. Truman made this their "oval study," using a desk presented to the White House by Queen Victoria during the Hayes Administration. Now used by President Reagan in the West Wing Oval Office, the desk was made from timbers of the H.M.S. *Resolute,* a British ship saved by American whalers in the Arctic after it was abandoned during a rescue mission in 1854.

Today, the Yellow Oval Room serves as a formal drawing room for the President and his family and as a reception room for foreign visitors attending state dinners and luncheons. The room gives access to the Truman Balcony. Overlooking the South Lawn, the balcony offers a panorama of the Ellipse, the Washington Monument, and the Jefferson Memorial. Many First Families have used the balcony for dining, entertaining guests, and viewing Fourth of July fireworks.

"Cliffs of Green River, Wyoming," painted in 1909-10 by American artist Thomas Moran, hangs to the left of the mantel. Moran's use of lush colors and his stylistic treatment of light and atmosphere reflect the influence of his teacher, the English romantic painter J.M.W. Turner. Moran accompanied several geological expeditions to unexplored regions of the West. His landscapes provided dramatic records of these wild areas.

Displayed in the President's Dining Room are a wine bucket dating from the Monroe Administration and pieces from a French silver service purchased by President Jackson for the White House in 1833.

THE PRESIDENT'S DINING ROOM

The President's Dining Room, which serves as a convenient place for family meals and private entertainment, is furnished in the styles of the American Federal period. Draperies of blue and green silk damask with gold-fringed green silk valances and a Turkish Hereke rug were chosen to complement the historical wallpaper.

Until it was converted into a dining room in 1961, this large northwest room on the second floor had been used as a family bedroom or sitting room. In the 19th century, it served as a bedroom for children of Presidents, including Tad Lincoln, and for relatives, such as Mr. and Mrs. Andrew Jackson Donelson. President and Mrs. Grover Cleveland and also President and Mrs. William McKinley used the room as their bedroom. Alice Roosevelt Longworth recalled that it was in this room that her appendix was removed.

Most of the American Federal furniture in the room was given to the White House in 1961 and 1962, including the Sheraton pedestal dining table and the New York Sheraton chairs, which are like those in the Family Dining Room on the State Floor. A Hepplewhite hunt table with silver drawer pulls stands between the windows.

Once owned by Daniel Webster, the American mahogany sideboard on the west wall bears his initials "D. W." inside an unusual front pull-out desk section decorated with finely inlaid satinwood stars and an eagle. On the sideboard stand pieces from a French silver dessert service and one of Monroe's oval tureens. The dessert service and a silver dinner service were bought by Andrew Jackson for the White House in 1833 from the Russian Minister Baron de Tuyll and carry the mark of a noted French goldsmith, Martin Biennais. Jackson was sharply criticized at the time for spending more than $4,000 in federal funds for the silver services, although it is now recognized that the money was well spent.

On the east wall, a plaster composition mantel designed about 1815 by Robert Welford of Philadelphia bears the famous words spoken by Commodore Oliver Perry after the Battle of Lake Erie, during the War of 1812: "We have met the enemy, and they are ours."

Above the mantel hangs a gilded girandole mirror probably made in New York about 1820. To the right of the fireplace is an American card table with its date of manufacture—1788—inlaid on the apron. A small mahogany sideboard attributed to the Annapolis cabinetmaker John Shaw stands to the right of the entrance to the hall.

The wallpaper in this room, called "The War of Independence," is a later version of the 1834 Zuber paper in the Diplomatic Reception Room. American landscapes, based on engravings made in the 1820's by Engelmann, form the background for the somewhat fanciful scenes of the Revolution. To the left of the windows, General Washington triumphantly enters Boston in 1776. (The State House, which appears on the city skyline, was not in fact completed until 1798.) Between the windows is an imaginary battle near Virginia's Natural Bridge.

THE WEST SITTING HALL

Filled with personal belongings from the Reagans' California home, the West Sitting Hall serves as a private living room for the First Family. The cheery red—Mrs. Reagan's favorite color—of the upholstery brightens the room, even though frost clouds the fan window. The Chinese porcelain objects on the table in the foreground were collected by Mrs. Reagan.

The West Sitting Hall, overlooking the West Wing and the Executive Office Building, was little more than a glorified stair landing until the renovation of 1902. During the 19th century this area was as sparsely furnished as the main hall. Occasionally a detail caught the attention of a visitor or reporter—a special correspondent in the Hayes Administration singled out the "RICH BUT FRIGHTFULLY UGLY CARPET."

After 1902 the hall became a private sitting area; successive Presidential families furnished it with favorite items of their own to re-create the atmosphere of home. Eleanor Roosevelt closed off the west hall with screens and ordered bright chintz slipcovers for the sofas and chairs; her social secretary considered it "really the most cheery and comfortable spot in the White House." This was where the family gathered for afternoon tea and where Mrs. Roosevelt presided over the traditional morning coffee with family and staff members and guests. During the Truman renovation of 1948-52, the architects turned the hall into a room by enclosing it with solid partitions.

On the north wall of the West Sitting Hall hangs "The Forest" (left), one of eight paintings by the 19th-century French artist Paul Cézanne bequeathed to the United States Government in 1952 "for the adornment of the White House." Cézanne sought to reintroduce an element of structure to the sensuous and color-dominated style of fellow Impressionists.

THE WEST WING

Well before the end of the 19th century, it had become clear that the cramped quarters of the second floor of the White House were no longer adequate for the offices of the President and his staff. An additional disadvantage was the lack of privacy for the Presidential family.

To solve the problem, Congress appropriated $65,196 for the construction of the West Wing in 1902. The architectural firm of McKim, Mead & White, under considerable pressure from President Theodore Roosevelt to complete the addition rapidly, proposed a modest temporary structure that would complement the mansion; the problem of building "a permanent, adequate, and thoroughly dignified office" was to be settled later.

In fact, the West Wing has remained at its original site although it was doubled in size in 1909 and further enlarged in 1927 and 1934. Additional offices for the Vice President and executive personnel are located to the west of the White House in the ornate Executive Office Building, begun during Grant's term of office to house the State, War, and Navy Departments. The remodeling of the West Wing in 1969 added a new driveway and portico on the north side, which provided a more formal entrance and reception area for the President's callers.

The foyer leading to the West Wing Reception Room contains a small equestrian statue, a miniature of the Clark Mills statue of Andrew Jackson in Lafayette Park. Purchased for the White House in 1857, it bears the stamp of Cornelius and Baker of Philadelphia.

THE WEST WING RECEPTION ROOM: Also called the Appointments Lobby, this room was created in 1969 from the former Press Lobby. Between two sofas copied from an original piece in the Governor's Palace in Williamsburg stands a late 18th-century English library bookcase that exhibits porcelain bird figures. On the west wall hangs a large gallery clock; carved and gilded, it was made in 1810 by Simon Willard of Roxbury, Massachusetts.

Displayed in the room are American landscape paintings of the mid-19th century. On the right above the sofa hangs "The Last of the Mohicans," dated 1857 and signed by the Hudson River School artist Asher B. Durand, and on the left, Worthington Whittredge's "Crossing the River Platte." Initially painting from field sketches, Whittredge reworked the scene to correct the appearance of the trees after making another trip west. This landscape emphasizes the flat expanse of the plain and the crystalline quality of the western air. "Cannonading on the Potomac," by A. Wordsworth Thompson, and "View of the City of Washington from the Anacostia Shore," by William McLeod, are also in the room.

The West Wing Reception Room (below) contains three major American landscape paintings. Worthington Whittredge's "Crossing the River Platte," painted about 1868, hangs to the left of the breakfront bookcase; to the right is "The Last of the Mohicans," completed in 1857 by Asher B. Durand. A still life by William Michael Harnett hangs near the Durand painting.

"Point Lobos, Monterey, California," painted in 1912 by Thomas Moran, bears the artist's thumbprint in the lower right corner.

A still life by William Michael Harnett, entitled "Cincinnati Enquirer, 1888," hangs on the west wall. This painting demonstrates Harnett's mastery of the style known as trompe l'oeil, which means "to fool the eye." He captures for the imagination a man's comfortable activity in his study by capturing for the eye the aftermath of that activity as reflected in the objects left on a table. On the north wall hangs Thomas Moran's 1912 "Point Lobos, Monterey, California."

Also on display in the reception room is a 19th-century copy of a Gilbert Stuart portrait of John Adams. This was the official White House portrait of Adams until 1986, when a life portrait by John Trumbull was acquired and hung in the Blue Room.

The West Wing Reception Room today bears little resemblance to the Press Lobby that was located here from the early 1900's to the late 1960's. During those years, the room was usually filled with reporters and photographers sitting and reading in large, worn leather armchairs and sofas—or racing to their telephones when a White House news story broke. Current arrangements give the news media space in the area connecting the West Wing and the mansion, where temporary flooring was laid over the indoor swimming pool.

THE ROOSEVELT ROOM: Staff meetings and occasional press conferences take place in the Roosevelt Room. Its former name, the Fish Room, was acquired during the time of Franklin D. Roosevelt, when it contained an aquarium and mementos of the President's fishing trips. Roosevelt's staff, however, nicknamed the room "the morgue" because so many callers sat "cooling off" in it. President Kennedy continued the Fish Room decor, displaying a mounted sailfish on one wall.

The Roosevelt Room, furnished with Queen Anne and Chippendale reproductions and warmed by a blazing fire on wintry days, provides a convenient place for meetings of all kinds. The mahogany breakfront bookcase, which stands against the west wall, was made for the White House in 1902. It contains bound volumes of Presidential papers. The carved wooden mantel on the east wall, installed in 1934, displays a bronze bust of Theodore Roosevelt, completed in 1910 by James Earle Fraser and given to the White House in 1971. Fraser also made the small bronze profile portrait exhibited in the room.

Above the mantel hangs "The Signing of the Declaration of Independence," sketched in oils between 1870 and 1880 by Edouard-Armand Dumaresque. Albert Bierstadt's "Looking up the Yosemite Valley," painted in 1863, hangs over the sofa on the north wall. The room also contains the gold medallion that was presented to Theodore Roosevelt in 1906, when he received the Nobel Peace Prize.

The two oil portraits of President Theodore Roosevelt displayed here were both painted about 1910. Tade Styka's dramatic equestrian portrait contrasts with Philip de László's head-and-shoulder representation. President Franklin D. Roosevelt is represented by Alfred Jonniaux's 1958 oil painting and a bronze plaque with a bas-relief portrait completed in 1933 by John De Stefano.

The Roosevelt Room, a staff meeting room formerly called the Fish Room, was named by President Nixon to honor Theodore Roosevelt, who made the West Wing a reality. Tade Styka painted the equestrian portrait of Theodore Roosevelt (right) in Paris about 1910.

**THE
WEST
WING**

THE CABINET ROOM: *Since 1902 the Cabinet has met in the West Wing.
This room, which looks out on the Rose Garden, has been used since 1934.
Cabinet meetings regularly include the Department Secretaries and
other officials appointed by the President. The room is also used for
National Security Council sessions, meetings with Congressional
leaders and Presidential advisers, and for special award presentations.*

The chairs, copies of a late 18th-century American style, bear brass plaques with Cabinet members' names. President Nixon purchased the mahogany pedestal conference table in 1970. Marble busts of George Washington and Benjamin Franklin rest on pedestals in niches flanking the fireplace. President Reagan chose for the room the portrait of Dwight D. Eisenhower by Thomas E. Stephens, which hangs over the mantel, as well as portraits of Jefferson, Lincoln, Taft, and Coolidge.

THE WEST WING

THE PRESIDENT'S OVAL OFFICE: The Chief Executive meets formally with visiting chiefs of state and heads of government in the Oval Office. Built in 1909, it was moved in 1934 from the center of the West Wing to its southeast corner. Architectural features of this spacious room include a handsomely proportioned cornice, pediments over the doors, lunettes above the French doors and above the west-wall niches, and a reproduction of the Presidential seal in low relief set into the ceiling.

The Oval Office reflects each change of administration more dramatically than any other area of the White House except the private quarters. Most Presidents fill the office with personal mementos or gifts, such as the photographs of family members and friends that President Reagan displays by the windows behind his desk.

President Reagan has chosen for the Oval Office the desk that Queen

Victoria presented to President Rutherford B. Hayes in 1880; it was made from the timbers of the H.M.S. *Resolute*. Other furnishings in the room are comfortable contemporary pieces, a number of antiques, and works of art such as Frederic Remington's "Bronco Buster," a bronze sculpture given to the White House in 1973. The oval rug, with turquoise rosettes on a pale gold ground and a Savonnerie-style border, was specially designed for this room.

Matching antique Chinese covered vases adorn the marble mantel; above the mantel hangs a portrait of George Washington in dress uniform, painted by Charles Willson Peale, father of the noted Peale family of artists. Executed in 1776 for a "French gentleman," this painting is thought to be the only replica of a life portrait painted by Peale earlier that year. The background commemorates the siege of Boston, which ended on March 17, 1776, when British troops withdrew from the city; it was General Washington's first victory of the Revolution. On either side of the mantel are scenes of 19th-century America.

Above a Massachusetts card table to the left of the windows hangs a painting entitled "The President's House," based on an engraving made in 1839. Outside the Oval Office lies the Rose Garden, where many important Presidential guests are received.

The decor of the President's Oval Office may vary from one administration to another but the flags standing behind this desk remain in their traditional places: to the President's left, the Presidential flag; to his right, in the position of honor, the flag of the United States of America.

THE ROSE GARDEN: At the west end of the Rose Garden, French doors of the President's Oval Office open into a white-pillared colonnade similar in style to the adjoining west terrace pavilion, which connects the West Wing to the Executive Residence. Much as the Jacqueline Kennedy Garden on the east side of the mansion is frequently used by the First Lady to receive her guests, so the Rose Garden serves as a reception area for the President.

Visitors traditionally welcomed there include foreign dignitaries and Medal of Honor recipients. The first team of U. S. astronauts and the first woman to be appointed to the Supreme Court of the United States were also received in the Rose Garden. It is used for occasional press conferences and has served as the setting for elegant state dinners, as in 1976 during the Bicentennial visit of Queen Elizabeth II of Great Britain and, more recently, for the 1986 visit of Brazilian President José Sarney. The Rose Garden was the scene of the first outdoor White House wedding when Tricia Nixon was married to Edward Cox in June 1971.

Roses were first planted here by Ellen Axson Wilson in 1913. Except for some alterations during the enlargement of the West Wing in 1934 and the renovation of the mansion between 1948 and 1952, no signifi-

*The Rose Garden follows
the plan of a traditional
18th-century American
garden. Planting beds,
with flowering crab
apples placed at intervals,
form the long lines of the
rectangle, framed by
hedges of osmanthus
and boxwood. Springtime
brings a profusion of
tulips, grape hyacinths,
and columbine to the
garden. As these fade,
roses, anemones, and
other summer flowers
take their place; autumn
flowers—heliotrope,
chrysanthemums, and
salvia—then provide
color until frost.*

cant changes were made until 1962 when, at the request of President
Kennedy, the Rose Garden was redesigned by Mrs. Paul Mellon.

As early as 1800, the first White House garden was being planned for
President John Adams. A Washingtonian recorded in a diary on March
20 of that year: "After breakfast we walked . . . to the ground behind the
President's House, which [will be] enclosed and laid out for a garden. It
is at present in great confusion, having on it old brick kilns, pits to con-
tain Water used by the brick makers. . . ." The writer failed to mention
the type of garden planned for this area.

By 1902, forcing beds, greenhouses, and conservatories, constructed
in the second half of the 19th century, occupied the site on the grounds
selected for the new West Wing. The demolition of the "glass houses"
uncovered a large part of Thomas Jefferson's 1807 west pavilion. The
original construction, which had been incorporated into the understruc-
ture of a Victorian greenhouse, was strengthened and made a part of
the new west pavilion. This restoration and the rebuilding of the east
pavilion, which had been pulled down in 1869, clearly underscore the
efforts of Theodore Roosevelt and the architects of the West Wing to
maintain the original character and plan of the historic mansion.

*F6

F7

*F9

*F8

*F5

*F3

*F2

F4

G6

G5

*G2

G4

A cutaway view of the White House—with the South Portico in the foreground—reveals the mansion's interior. Visitors who take the public guided tour walk along the glass-enclosed colonnade to the Ground Floor Corridor, climb the stairs to the four state reception rooms and the State Dining Room on the first floor, then depart by way of the North Entrance.

Ground Floor
G1   Library
*G2   Ground Floor Corridor
G3   Vermeil Room
G4   China Room
G5   Diplomatic Reception Room
G6   Map Room

First Floor
*F1   East Room
*F2   Green Room
*F3   Blue Room
F4   South Portico
*F5   Red Room
*F6   State Dining Room
F7   Family Dining Room
*F8   Cross Hall
*F9   Entrance Hall

*An asterisk marks rooms
 open to the public.*

ROBERT W. NICHOLSON

II

THE CHANGING
WHITE HOUSE

"Long live George Washington, President of the United States!" A cheering crowd in front of Federal Hall in New York City hailed the man who had just taken an oath of office—blending the ancient salutation to a king and the new title for a new kind of executive.

Thus for decades old forms and new experiments would shape the life of a nation. In 1789 the United States of America began working out a second try at self-government under the new Constitution; and this, for a free people, meant a variety of undertakings: from passing new laws to paving the streets of a capital city, and agreeing on republican manners for a President's dinner party.

By July 12, 1790, President Washington was signing an Act of Congress to fix Philadelphia as temporary capital until the "first Monday in December, 1800," when the federal government would take up residence in a district "not exceeding ten miles square . . . on the river Potomac." After long wrangling over a location, Secretary of State Thomas Jefferson and Secretary of the Treasury Alexander Hamilton had bargained their way to a supper-table agreement that Congress would approve.

Ten years may have seemed more than adequate for preparing the Capital. It wasn't. Not until mid-March 1792 did the three Commissioners of the Federal City set up competitions for the design of a building for the Congress and a house for the President, with Jefferson writing an announcement for the newspapers.

George Washington takes the oath of office as first President at Federal Hall in New York City on April 30, 1789. Although he had selected the site for the White House and approved its design, he never lived there.

While the government remained in New York, the remodeled City Hall provided space for Congress, and the first Chief Executive lived in rented houses. A handsome Georgian residence intended for President and Mrs. Washington was unfinished when the move to Philadelphia took place in 1790; once there the President occupied a house owned by Robert Morris.

For the permanent buildings in the "Federal City"—as he modestly called it—Washington wanted "size, form, and elegance" looking "beyond the present day." But for early use, he thought, builders should put up an Executive Mansion suited to the time, and leave anything more to the future when the country would surely be richer, larger, more populous, and more important in the world. When the Dublin-trained builder James Hoban won his $500 prize and commission to erect the President's House, Washington suggested that he omit a third story.

Although Washington generously called the assorted designs submitted a credit to architecture in an infant republic, most of them were more gallant than skilled. Hoban's design (see pages 108-9) stood out in competence, originality, and practicality—he included a plan, eventually discarded, for wings to be added when necessary. His unusual "elliptic saloon," today the Blue Room, has drawn admiring comment for generations.

In supervising construction, Hoban met varied and complex frustrations, as did his counterpart Dr. William Thornton, who was struggling to get the Capitol ready. Skilled hands for such enterprises were few; free workmen apparently avoided an area where slave labor kept wages low. Sales of lots in the District of Columbia lagged. Congress economized on appropriations. Materials brought by water came slowly upriver as wind and tide favored the ships.

By June 1800, when 131 federal employees arrived with their accumulated papers and President John Adams came to visit a city of 501 households, neither the "Congress house" nor the "President's Palace" was complete. Thinking that one man could certainly find lodging somewhere, the harried commissioners had stopped work on the "Palace" the year before to concentrate on the Capitol. Its north wing was available when legislators straggled into town in November, and Adams found shelter if not comfort at the mansion.

His wife, Abigail, during the first weeks of occupancy, penned candid letters to her daughter, listing the problems of a house on such "a grand and superb scale." Not a single bell to summon a servant—officials had scrabbled desperately to procure these, without success. No firewood, in a region of forests—"because people cannot be found to cut and cart it!"—and raw winter weather. Of the six rooms she called "comfortable" and described, none was her own. With some justice she thought New Englanders would have done a better job of finishing things. Meanwhile, she warned, her daughter should keep all these

Time-darkened silver of this Chippendale looking glass reflected the Washingtons while they stayed in the Morris home.

During his term of office, President and Mrs. Washington lived in this Philadelphia house owned by financier Robert Morris. Earlier, when New York was the capital, they first occupied a brick house on Cherry Street, then a residence on Broadway. In both cities houses built for the President were completed too late for the Washingtons to use them. John Adams, who also passed much of his term in Philadelphia, prized this graceful coffee urn of Sheffield silver plate.

Abigail Adams and her husband John became the first residents of the White House in November 1800, even though the mansion was still under construction.

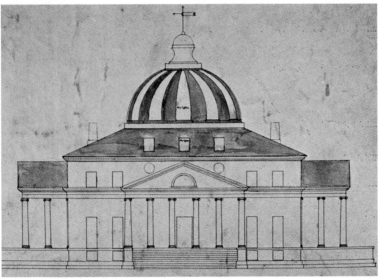

Final design for the President's House (above) was drawn in the mid-1790's by Irish architect James Hoban. He added an American eagle in the pediment to such traditional features as a hipped roof, balustrade, and arches alternating with triangles above the windows. Another effort in the same style appears at lower left, a design submitted by James Diamond of Maryland. "A. Z." entered the sophisticated plan above it, for many years thought to be the

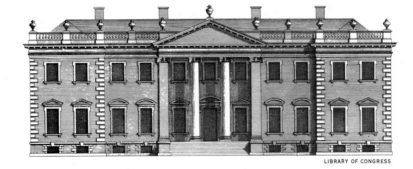

work of Thomas Jefferson. He turned to the Italian Renaissance architect Palladio for inspiration; others followed such designs as that at right center from James Gibbs's 1728 Book of Architecture, *most popular builder's guide of the 18th century. Its idiom survives in Irish mansions like Leinster House (upper right) and at the Château de Rastignac in southwest France, where an oval portico resembles the one Hoban added to the White House in 1824.*

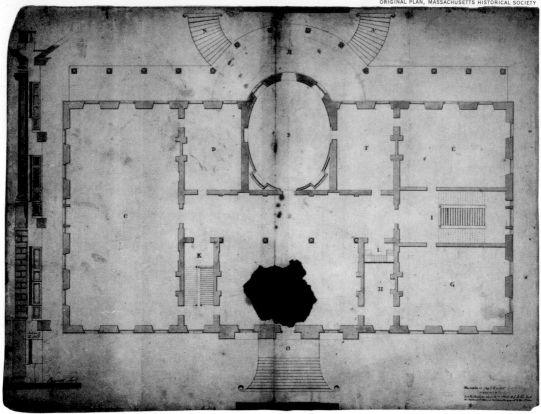

James Hoban, architect and builder of the White House, drew the plan for the State Floor (above) in his bid for the commission. It includes a portico and a colonnade that was never constructed.

complaints secret and quote her as saying only that "the situation is beautiful, which is true."

Undoubtedly Mrs. Adams meant the general vicinity, since the grounds of the mansion were a disreputable jumble of old kilns and water-filled pits for brickmaking, stonecutters' shacks, sheds for supplies, rubbish, and mud.

On November 15 the commissioners hired one James Clarke to get the back stairs and a privy built within a fortnight, and then to complete the interior doors and the grand window at the east end of the house. Evidently, when the lady of the White House had laundry hung up to dry in the East Room, it flapped in winter winds.

According to an inventory taken February 26, 1801, the Adamses had a fair amount of furniture at their disposal. The President's bed had white dimity curtains; his "dressing" mirror was "in tolerable order." Solid silver plate included two large "punch urns" with ladles and five dozen teaspoons; 33 pairs of sheets were "generally good," three "Table setts" of china complete. And the stables housed an "Elegant Chariot," a "Good Coachee," a "Market Waggon," and "7 Well looking Horses, chiefly advanced in years."

After four months of shivering in their chilly "castle," offering the most ceremonious hospitality possible under the circumstances, after weeks of uncertainty before the House of Representatives settled an electoral tie between Thomas Jefferson and Aaron Burr for President,

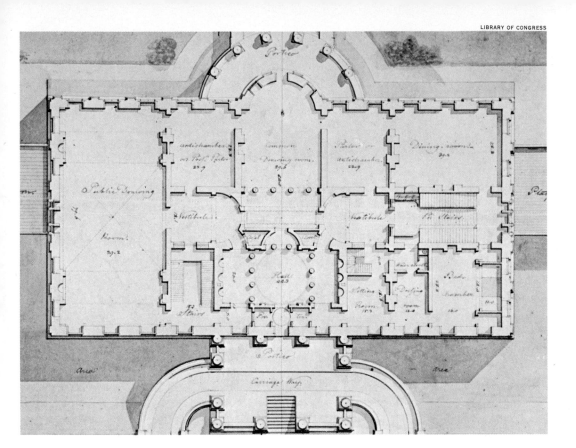

English-born architect Benjamin Henry Latrobe submitted the above plan to Jefferson in 1807. It proposed porticoes and pavilions, and a modification of rooms on the State Floor that was never executed.

the first residents of the White House were free to leave Washington.

An unfinished house was unlikely to annoy Jefferson, who had happily spent years remodeling Monticello, but he waited until March 19 before moving from a boardinghouse near the Capitol into his sandstone mansion. Then, as the first President to spend a full term there, he began his efforts to improve it and furnish it in style. The worst of the junk was carted out of the grounds and a post-and-rail fence erected. Instead of finding their way up wooden steps to the oval room that had been serving as a vestibule, guests picked their way up wooden steps to the north entrance. The principal staircase inside the mansion was not completed until the middle of Jefferson's first term.

In 1803, amateur architect Jefferson named professional architect Benjamin Henry Latrobe "Surveyor of the Public Buildings," and soon Latrobe was planning a new roof for the White House. So much rainwater had leaked through that the ceiling of the East Room had collapsed. Under the load of ill-fitting slates, the front and back walls of the mansion had started to spread. Latrobe substituted sheet iron, sparing the structure an estimated 82 tons, and secured the walls "by strong ties of Iron."

To provide space for household and official work, Jefferson designed low-lying pavilions east and west of the mansion; Latrobe completed these in 1807, building a fireproof vault for the Treasury at the far end of the east colonnade. That same year he planned a semicircular portico

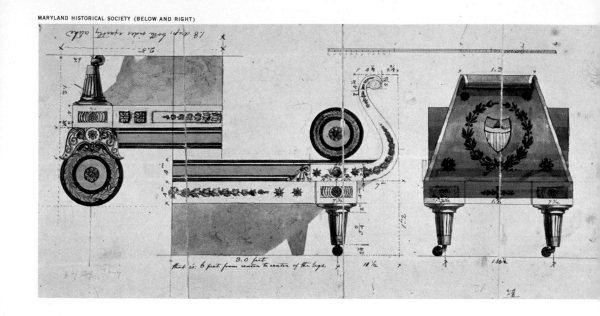

Latrobe, named Surveyor of Public Buildings by Jefferson in 1803, not only made changes on the exterior of the White House but also designed furniture for it. His drawing of the south façade (lower right) included pavilions and terraces completed in 1807. Latrobe's rendering of the east elevation shows the North Portico, finished in 1829, and the South Portico, completed in 1824. Latrobe began his collaboration in 1809 with the new

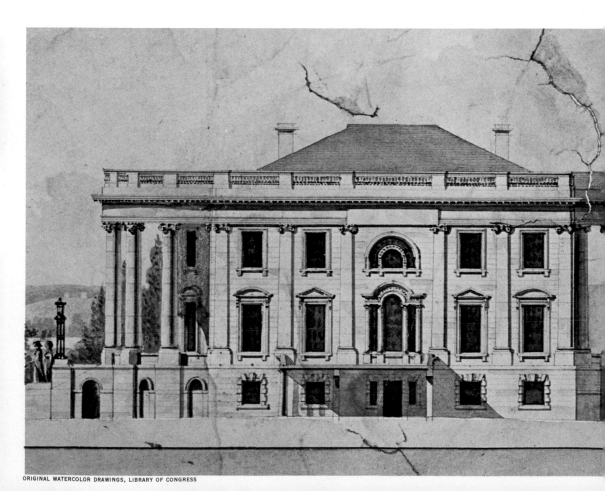

lady of the mansion, Dolley Madison, to decorate the "Oval Drawing
Room" (today's Blue Room) in the mode of the classic revival. He based
the 36 painted and gilded cane-seat chairs on the klismos—a chair of
Greek design; he adapted the triclinium—a couch used by Romans for
reclining at meals—for two sofas and four window seats (above left).
All were lost when the British burned the mansion on August 24, 1814.

for the south front of the house and a larger one, with a porte cochere —carriage porch—for the north. Jefferson approved these at once, but the first was not finished until 1824, the second five years later; both seem to include elements of Hoban's original design.

Although Jefferson's modifications to the White House progressed slowly, his changes in Presidential etiquette began in March 1801. Washington and Adams had favored a stately formality in the 18th-century mold of public dignity, praised by their admirers as upholding the greatness of America and denounced by their critics as savoring of monarchy. President Jefferson introduced a dramatic informality, acclaimed by his followers as true to the genius of the republic and scorned by his enemies as cheap in the debased fashion of French radicals. He sometimes came to the door in his slippers; he seated no one by precedence at his dinners—but if this infuriated diplomats, it cost few votes. Between these extremes, subsequent Presidents have adapted the usage of the White House to the changing customs of the country, while the public watched their restoration of a seemly order or their innovations toward a welcome ease.

For all his democratic manners, Jefferson furnished the White House in sumptuous style. He liked furniture "in the antique taste"—the classical revival manner with the crisp lines and cool restraint represented in France by the style now designated Louis XVI and in America by the term Federal. An inventory of 1809 distinguished mahogany pieces from the "fashionable" ones, with gilding and paint in crimson, green, blue, or black. Jefferson ignored precedent by draping many windows not in damask or brocade but in fashionable bright chintz. Unfortunately, it seems that none of his many guests—no artist, no drawing master, no cultivated person—so much as sketched any of his rooms or furnishings.

When that incomparable hostess Dolley Madison undertook to redecorate the mansion, shortly after her husband's inauguration in 1809, she asked Latrobe to design furniture for the "Oval Drawing Room." He drew chairs "to a Grecian Model," with sofas and settees "to match the same." They were made by John and Hugh Finlay of Baltimore. Latrobe's drawings survive (pages 112-13), and their muted tints help explain his wail of anguish when he saw the crimson velvet bought for cushions and draperies: "The curtains! Oh the terrible velvet curtains! Their effect will ruin me entirely so brilliant will they be."

In fact the room seemed entirely elegant when the Madisons received callers there on New Year's Day, 1810; contemporary accounts praised it highly. In 1813 young Elbridge Gerry, Jr., son of the Vice President, found it "immense and magnificent"; its curtains—"which cost 4$ a yard"—struck him as "superb."

This elegance was short-lived; barely a year later the British burned the White House. On August 23, while the President was off with an ill-trained army, Mrs. Madison packed a carriage load of Cabinet papers

Fire-darkened and crumbling, the White House stands desolate in 1816, beyond St. John's Church (also designed by Latrobe). The Madisons spent the last of his term in rented quarters—first Col. John Tayloe's Octagon House, then a smaller residence nearby.

Relics from the years of ruin: This writing-arm Windsor chair was used by Madison on the night of August 26, 1814, as he sat dispatching messages to his Cabinet from the Quaker town of Brookeville, Maryland. His medicine chest was taken from the mansion by a British soldier; a Canadian descendant returned it in 1939. A tea box from 1811, acquired in 1971, contains wallpaper ascribed by descendants of Latrobe to "the drawing room of the President's House"—possibly the White House.

FRANKLIN D. ROOSEVELT LIBRARY,
HYDE PARK, NEW YORK

WHITE HOUSE COLLECTION

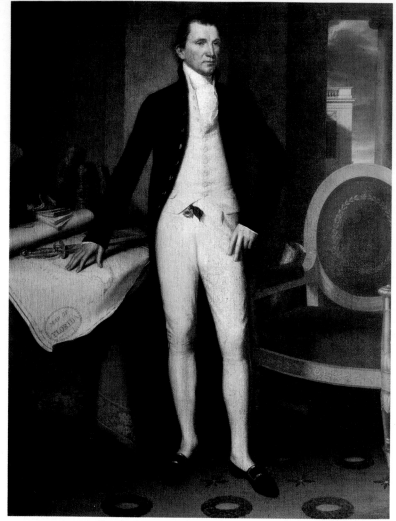

*His official home
restored, James Monroe
stands in the oval
drawing room by one of
the 38 chairs made for
him in 1817 by Pierre-
Antoine Bellangé of
Paris, cabinetmaker to the
rulers of France.*
*A superb pier table from
the same group, adorned
with carved and gilded
branches of olive, now
stands in the Entrance
Hall; it never left the
mansion. Baroness Hyde
de Neuville, wife of the
French Minister, sketched
an 1820 view of the
White House with its
neighboring office
buildings (below).*
*From left: Departments
of State, Treasury,
War, and Navy.*

By 1848 gas lamps lit Pennsylvania Avenue in front of the White House, as
shown in a lithograph (above) based on a watercolor by Augustus Köllner.
This scene, entitled "President's House," depicts the view from Lafayette Square.

into trunks; the next day she continued a letter to her sister, writing "within sound of the cannon! Mr. Madison comes not; may God protect him!" Someone procured a wagon; she ordered the government's silver put into it. She insisted on taking "the large picture of Gen. Washington. . . . I have ordered the frame to be broken, and the canvas taken out; it is done. . . . When I shall again write to you, or where I shall be tomorrow, I cannot tell!!" That night, August 24, the flames of the blazing mansion and Capitol raged against the sky until a summer downpour quenched them, leaving the dank smell of burned ruin.

Even after the treaty of peace, Washingtonians feared that Congress might decide to move the Capital to some safer place; and when the decision to remain was clear, rebuilding for the legislature took priority. The Madisons lived for a year in Col. John Tayloe's mansion, Octagon House, then in a smaller house on Pennsylvania Avenue.

Hoban took charge of his crumbling mansion, stripping out fire-damaged stone and brick and rebuilding the exterior walls. By mid-September 1817 the White House was habitable again, and Congress had appropriated $20,000 for furnishings alone. James Monroe had acquired valuable Louis XVI furniture as a diplomat in Paris; he sold this, with china and plate, to the government—and his agent muddled the transactions so badly that the matter was never fully untangled. To supplement his private collection and some used items of good quality that had been bought for the Madisons, Monroe ordered an array of goods from France for the oval drawing room, a parlor, a card room, and the dining room. He also bought American furniture; William King of Georgetown charged $1,584 in one bill for 24 chairs (one pictured opposite) and 4 sofas.

Filled with patriotic pride and curiosity, a throng arrived on January 1, 1818, to see the President's House in its new splendor. In the oval room where the Chief Magistrate stood, gilded Empire furniture from Bellangé of Paris (pages 46-47, 50, 51) shone in light playing from the hearth and the 50-candle chandelier. Ornaments of porcelain and silver, vermeil and gilded bronze (pages 36, 59) glittered on mantels and tables; on fine silks the sheen was still undimmed.

From that day to this, items from the Monroe restoration have formed the heart of the historic collection of the White House—with the one treasured exception known to have belonged to the mansion since 1800: the Gilbert Stuart portrait of George Washington (page 37) that Dolley Madison rescued from looting or destruction. One piece of the Bellangé furniture never left the collection—the pier table now in the Entrance Hall. But as recently as 1946, the remainder of the suite and most of Monroe's American pieces seemed beyond retrieving.

Throughout the 19th century, the residents of the White House furnished it in the current style whenever possible. They wanted the fashionable, the up-to-date, the modern, the changing finery of a fast-changing country. They made the best of what they inherited from

French artistry, 1817: one of a pair of fruit baskets wrought in bronze-doré. Bought for the dining room, each arrived with detachable branches to hold six candles.

former administrations, and thriftily, matter-of-factly, sold it at public auction as it grew outmoded and worn.

Yellowing accounts indicate some of the sums realized this way; but what became of which piece of furniture, at which sale and when, is seldom a matter of record.

Appropriations to keep the White House presentable were routine if not adequate, but a President with substantial opposition in Congress could expect trouble over household issues. Opponents of John Adams kicked up trouble with charges that he bought his seven "Well looking Horses" with money earmarked for furniture. His son John Quincy Adams, elected in 1824 with a minority of the popular vote, met a similar fuss over the private purchase of a billiard table and never did succeed in getting money enough to furnish the East Room.

And White House furnishings take hard wear, if not downright abuse. From one administration to the next, superb velvet curtains, elegant green silks, rich handwoven carpets pass from the freshness of a New Year's Day to the terse judgments of the man taking inventory: "in tolerable order . . . injured . . . more than half worn . . . much worn . . ." to the final "worn out." By March 24, 1825, a clerk reported that Monroe's purchases, "having been seven years or upwards, in use," were "of necessity more or less injured and defaced, notwithstanding the utmost care and attention. . . ." The portion collected for the Madisons in 1814 had become "altogether useless."

Not only changes in usefulness but also changes in equipment for American households — changes in technology and standards of comfort — come to life in White House records. The 1825 survey finds in a private room "one set yellow silk dome bed curtains" for "one elegant mahogany gilt mounted bedstead" with "one husk mattress" — the delicate sibilance of silk is answered in the harsher rustle of cornshucks.

Local artistry, 1817: one of 24 chairs that Monroe bought for the East Room from William King, cabinetmaker of Georgetown.

Much louder but with a similar change of key, the inauguration of Andrew Jackson spoke of a triumph for the frontier and political democracy. "Old Hickory," Hero of New Orleans, commanded the admiration of citizens with no time for polish — or veneer — and persons of gentility feared the mob would reign.

In fact, Jackson took pains to embellish the Executive Mansion. Long-deferred work on the North Portico got under way at once. For the first time a President was in a position to furnish the East Room; it was promptly done. To replace glass chipped and shattered since 1817, a Pittsburgh firm supplied a copious shipment costing $1,451.75 which included 12 dozen "richest cut" tumblers and 18 dozen wineglasses. A French porcelain dinner service of 440 pieces and a dessert set of 412 pieces came to $2,500. After eight years of high-toned entertaining and full-throated politics, General Jackson retired, still a popular hero.

His protégé Martin Van Buren had the bad luck to face not just a

President Andrew Jackson, portrayed by Ralph Earl, sits with stiff but formidable dignity in one of the Bellangé chairs. Like Jefferson, Jackson lived by a standard of ease and elegance that never cost him popular support. At far right, a print by George Cruikshank caricatures the crowd at a Jackson reception as "The President's Levee, or all Creation going to the White House." By Jackson's time the mansion's reception rooms were jammed even on routine occasions; the local population was passing 30,000. Below, a detail of George Cooke's 1833 painting shows Washington from across the Anacostia River.

financial panic and the worst depression the country had suffered to date, but the canniest Congressman who ever made fun of White House furbelows. On April 14, 1840, Representative Charles Ogle of Pennsylvania rose in the House to attack the "regal splendor of the Presidential palace." The President was a Democrat, Ogle a Whig. With appropriations acts, bills, and vouchers for evidence, he lambasted details from dwarf walls on the grounds to "ice cream vases" and bracket lights. Deftly he implied that other Presidents' purchases were Van Buren's doing. Ogle made great play with the satin medallion and galloon and gimp at windows in the "Blue Elliptical Saloon." After presenting Van Buren as a sissified spendthrift, he ridiculed him as a skinflint, making the plain farmers, poor laborers, and honest mechanics of America pay for cobweb brushes, churn and milk strainers, and the hemming of 12 dozen dishrags at the "pitiful price" of 50 cents per dozen.

Van Buren had spent less than Jackson. Even a few Whigs pointed out distortions in Ogle's ruthless comedy. Van Buren lost the election.

On a storm tide of hard cider and ballyhoo, William Henry Harrison won the Presidency, began his purchases for the mansion, took the oath of office, fell ill within a month, and died. The first President to die in office, he left his running mate John Tyler to take up the burdens of the executive branch with minimal support in Cabinet and Congress. As the latter refused Tyler's plea for additional funds for the White House, its furnishings rapidly approached dilapidation.

Upholstered only once since 1817, the chairs reached a condition of "perfect explosion at every prominent point that presents contact with the outer garments of the visitors." Those in the East Room, said one journal, would disgrace a house of shame.

I n 1845, the James K. Polks' first year in the mansion, money for furnishings became available again. Victorian fancy took charge — walnut frames, purple plush, rockers in green figured plush for the Red Room, 24 "Gothic" chairs — an early instance of the vogue for revivals that pilfered the styles of various ages in rapid succession.

New amenities appeared: payment of $25 for a "Refregrator" (icebox) was authorized in 1845; gas lights were installed in 1849. Older amenities were maintained. On June 30, 1849, early in President Zachary Taylor's term, someone fitted a carpet in the water closet, charging 50 cents. An attic cistern for rainwater had supplied a water closet in Jefferson's time; running water from a city system dated only from Jackson's.

Although Hoban had added 12 new fireplaces in 1817 and Van Buren had installed a furnace, heating remained a problem. Franklin Pierce had the benefit not only of a bathroom but also of an improved heating plant to make the mansion more comfortable.

Perhaps no President was better suited to preside comfortably at the Executive Mansion than James Buchanan, the dignified bachelor

In a painting full of careful portraits (attributed to Francis B. Carpenter), President and Mrs. Lincoln honor Gen. Ulysses S. Grant shortly before his appointment in March 1864 to head all the Union armies. Costly fabrics chosen by Mary Lincoln to refurbish the mansion suffered damage during the war years, when visitors cut or tore souvenirs from draperies, furniture, and even rugs.

who once described himself as "an old public functionary." With the poised help of his niece Harriet Lane, who acted as hostess, he entertained often and genially. In 1857 Congress allotted $5,000 to buy portraits of five former Presidents, plus a routine $20,000 that paid for a new conservatory. For the Blue Room, where Monroe's furniture had stood since 1817, he ordered a rococo-revival suite that served for decades (pages 126-27); except for the large pier table, the Bellangé pieces were sold at auction.

With veteran aplomb Buchanan welcomed the first envoys from Japan; in the autumn of 1860 he received Queen Victoria's heir, Prince Edward, traveling for diplomatic reasons under the title of Baron Renfrew. The first royal houseguest made a great impression—for years thereafter people spoke of the "Prince of Wales room." (Today this room serves as the President's private dining room.)

Probably no President ever faced a crisis for which his abilities were less suited than Buchanan. The sectional dreads and suspicions that had challenged Monroe's tact, Jackson's fire, (Continued on page 128)

*Earliest known photograph of the East Room (above), from
1861, shows the King chairs, Jackson's chandeliers—converted
to gas—and a carpet from the Buchanan Administration. Grant's
redecoration in 1873 (below) resulted in decor hailed at the
time as "pure Greek" but later ridiculed as "steamboat Gothic."*

*Living green meant
luxury in the late
1890's. The vogue for
potted ferns and flowers,*

dating from Grover Cleveland's time, strained the timbers of the White House so severely by William McKinley's term that Army engineers propped up the East Room floor with stout posts before gala evenings. Here, cut velvet as intricate as foliage covers the circular ottoman.

In the Blue Room of 1867 (above), decorated by President Andrew
Johnson's married daughter Martha Patterson, geometrical forms accent
the contour of Hoban's "elliptic saloon." The gasolier dates from the
mid-19th century, the rococo-revival furniture from the Buchanan
Administration. Mrs. Patterson chose the blue paper with panels
bordered in black and gold. On New Year's Day, when the refurbished
parlor first went on show at the traditional public levee, the weather was
"most inclement"—muslin covers protected the velvet carpets. Two decades
later, during Cleveland's first term, the room (right) contains Louis C.
Tiffany's decor, introduced by President Arthur. A shield-and-star pattern
replaces the sweeping ovals of the ceiling. The delicate robin's egg tint
of the hand-pressed wallpaper was accented in ivory; in the rosettes
sparkled inlay of opaque or colored glass. From the mantel, below
Monroe's vases and Hannibal clock, hangs a new adornment: velvet fringe.

Taylor's stern obstinacy, and Fillmore's conciliation, increased during Buchanan's term and neared flash point with the election of Lincoln.

When the Lincolns moved into the White House, a tough group of Kansans joined Senator Jim Lane as "Frontier Guards," to patrol the porticoes with muskets, and drill or sleep in the East Room until loyal troops arrived to defend the Capital. "A sort of uncanny glamour seems to have been settling upon the city. . . ," wrote one of Lincoln's secretaries; "a strange and shuddering kind of thing, and its central, darkest, most bewildering witchcraft works around this Executive Mansion."

Whatever uncertainties hovered around it, Mary Lincoln meant to hold her own there and make it home. She put warm sheepskin rugs by the beds. Inevitably, visitors were finding the furniture "deplorably shabby." She selected new rosewood furniture, new velvet hassocks, new plush and brocatelle fabrics. She overran an appropriation by $6,700; the responsible official endorsed a wallpaper bill for the state floor *as selected by Mrs. Lincoln & not by Com. Pub. Bdgs.*"

Angrily Lincoln refused to ask for a deficiency appropriation: ". . . it would stink in the nostrils of the American people to have it said that the President of the United States had approved a bill overrunning an appropriation of $20 000 for *flub dubs* for this damned old house, when the soldiers cannot have blankets."

In former decades, foreigners had remarked that plain citizens at the White House controlled themselves with self-respecting good manners. However, a kind of hysterical vandalism marked the war years. A man was caught "skinning" satin damask from a sofa. Even as Congress was enacting deficiency bills for the mansion, its finery suffered.

Word-of-mouth tradition was keeping up with the mansion's heirlooms, more or less. Lincoln's secretary William O. Stoddard remembered the piece known as "Andrew Jackson's chair," presented to him

Lincoln's office and Cabinet Room as of October 1864: a detailed and invaluable sketch by C. K. Stellwagen. He noted that Lincoln's chair by the window was covered in black haircloth. Littering the Cabinet table are maps, books, and rolls of documents, including long letters endorsing many a plea for military rank or civil office. In a sketch published in 1877, office seekers crowd the mansion to see newly inaugurated President Rutherford B. Hayes.

by citizens of Mexico. A "unique mahogany frame" and "hollow morocco leather seat" made it "peculiarly comfortable." Legend had it that Jackson leaned back in it on winter evenings before the fireplace in his room, smoking his pipe and resting his stockinged feet on the middle bricks of the fireplace arch. "Mr. Lincoln expressed a wish to have those bricks preserved when the fireplace was reconstructed, but they were somehow mislaid and lost."

As for physical change, Lincoln made only a minor one, long since eliminated: a private passage on the second floor from the library through the reception room to his office. (Today it would run from the Yellow Oval Room through the Treaty Room to the Lincoln Bedroom.) Thus he could reach the private quarters unseen by waiting strangers. A contemporary called it "... his only monument in the building ... it tells a long story of duns and loiterers, contract-hunters and seekers for commissions, garrulous parents on paltry errands, toadies without measure and talkers without conscience."

Nasty eddies of bitterness followed the widowed Mary Lincoln from the mansion: charges that she had taken away public property. Indignantly she itemized things she had packed, gifts from humble Unionists: waxwork, country quilts, homemade chairs. Apparently no one really supervised the White House during the five weeks she lay mourning in her room, and vandals helped themselves. With official approval she had taken a shaving stand her husband had liked, leaving one of equal quality to replace it.

President Andrew Johnson, for all his troubles with Congress, received funds to decorate the house again, and President Ulysses S. Grant carried out a thorough renovation in 1873, at the height of the Gilded Age. Splendor aside, by now the White House was showing its years in ominous fashion. The Commissioner of Public Buildings

reported that a large ceiling had collapsed, "but fortunately when the room was unoccupied." Almost all the ceilings were cracked, and those in the state rooms had settled several inches. The basement he dismissed as "necessarily very damp and unhealthy."

He dwelt on the inconvenience of rigging up bridges from windows (page 138) when large receptions made it necessary to supplement the single entrance at the North Portico.

Closets, he noted, were "now considered indispensable," and the White House had none. (Nobody built closets in the 1790's, but the age of machinery—with its textile factories and sewing machines—had left chests inadequate for the greater quantities of apparel.) Counting the library, only eight rooms were available in the private quarters for family and guests. Everything considered, the commissioner thought "it hardly seems possible to state anything in favor of the house as a residence; but if 'thoroughly repaired,' it would serve its purpose admirably as an executive office."

Of course the White House continued, however clumsily, to serve both purposes at once. If national sentiment was the only factor to assure this, it was more than enough. A President with a small family, like Grover Cleveland, could count himself lucky, but nothing could be expected to shrink the volume of public business.

The callers who sought postal or military commissions from Lincoln were replaced by callers who sought pardons from Andrew Johnson or friendly agreements with Grant, and the paperwork never diminished. Arrangements for Reconstruction in the South and for fast-growing settlements in the West were increasing the number of government jobs, the scope of patronage, the hopeful ranks of applicants. Lobbyists —even a few soft-spoken women—moved suavely among the throng on the second floor, to speak in the interest of railroads or farmers, veterans or freedmen.

From deadlock in the national life to a note on the Red Room—so crisis dwindles when successfully outlived. Unique among Presidential elections, that of 1876 strained the Constitution to the point of frantic improvising. Democrat Samuel J. Tilden apparently edged ahead of Republican Rutherford B. Hayes in popular votes, with contested electoral votes in Oregon and three southern states. One of those electoral votes could put Tilden in the White House. Behind the scenes, Northerners and Southerners were bargaining. Congress named a special Electoral Commission. As a final complication, the lawful inauguration day—March 4—fell on a Sunday, and tradition deferred the ceremonies to Monday.

On February 20, 1877, Grant assumed the count was virtually settled. He invited the Hayeses to come to the mansion as guests on March 3. "Sinister rumors from W. [Washington] leave us in doubt. . . ," Hayes replied; they planned to stay with friends but would come to dinner— if declared successful. He was, by one vote, but apprehension of some kind of coup d'etat or violence still ran high.

Exotica and domestic luxury meet in the Harrisons' Red Room (left), the family parlor; a Tiffany mantel with tortoiseshell tiles; an Austrian fire-screen; Oriental vases and screens; crimson wallpaper with a "Moorish" frieze. In 1882 President Arthur had called on Louis Tiffany of New York to redecorate the mansion in the emerging style of Art Nouveau. The most famous installation was the stained-glass screen in the Cross Hall (below).

American eagle decorates a plate of the
Harrison china, made in Limoges, France.

Grant thought Hayes should take the oath of office in secret on Saturday, just in case. Reluctantly, Hayes agreed.

As guests assembled for a dinner of surpassing brilliance, Grant quietly slipped into the Red Room with Hayes and Chief Justice Morrison R. Waite. The oath administered, they quickly returned.

On Monday, amid swirls of rumor about the oath but no violence whatever, the public ceremonies took place with as much decorum as ever. Reporters fell back on the decor of the red parlor for mood or detail. "Its crimson fires fell upon them . . ." cried one; "Red mirrors of a darker red reflected the smouldering light of other mirrors. . . . a dark blood flush, enveloped them. . . . the consecrated and the priest went out together to the sound of merriment . . . the flash of gems in women's ears and the beards of o'erambitious men."

The room is "between the banquet hall and the violet blue Parlor," noted another journalist, and was newly furnished in "the English version of the Queen Anne." The Japanese Minister had presented two small Japanese cabinets. The writer faithfully described the fire screen as "a curious large gilt one with a worsted center piece," but did not mention that Austria was the donor.

In 1878 Hayes accepted the credentials of the first Chinese minister to the United States, in a private ceremony in the Blue Room. The Imperial diplomats wore their national costume, which always attracted attention at state dinners.

Of international gifts, probably none has given longer service than the desk presented to President Hayes, a token of goodwill from Great Britain. In 1854 the crew of H.M.S. *Resolute,* trapped in Arctic ice, had abandoned her; the Yankee whaler *George Henry* in 1855 freed the *Resolute* and brought her to port. The ship was bought, refitted, and given to Queen Victoria by President Pierce on behalf of the American people. Two decades later, the *Resolute* was broken up and Her Majesty had the desk made from the old ship's seasoned oak. Since then many Presidents have used it in their private studies or the Oval Office.

The White House staff—like the diplomatic corps—was growing. In 1881 a de facto "Bureau of Appointments"—seven persons counting the President's private secretary—had second-floor office space to cope with patronage demands raining down on James A. Garfield. That same year the shooting of the President by a disappointed office seeker brought demands for reform and led to establishment of the Civil Service in 1883.

Chester A. Arthur, whose urbane New York ways earned him the nickname "Elegant Arthur," inherited an Executive Mansion not at all to his taste. One nostalgic visitor had dismissed the furnishings as "modern abominations in upholstery and garish gilding" and the rooms as "staring, pretentious and Frenchy," preferring the quiet dignity of Lincoln's mahogany pieces in their port-wine plush. Arthur swept out innumerable abominations on April 15, 1882—24 wagonloads, by report, for the greatest "decayed furnishings" auction in White House annals. A crowd of 5,000 bid high for moth-eaten furniture from

Mrs. Benjamin Harrison, an avid painter of china, helped design the state service during her husband's administration. She also initiated the tradition of collecting state and family china of previous Presidents. Vast amounts of china were necessary for state dinners like the one below during the administration of Grover Cleveland. Meals often included 10 to 15 courses.

At the height of fashion: a guest bedroom in the Benjamin Harrison Administration. The "Lincoln" bed keeps its original cornice of gilt wood, with crown drapery of lace and fringed curtains. The marble-top center table was purchased with the bed, and the chairs beside the table probably were acquired at the same time. These, from a set of six, stood in a guest room during Andrew Johnson's term; four are in the Lincoln Sitting Room today. Possibly the same order included the chaise, or daybed, veiled by its afghan and dust ruffles. The massive wardrobe with mirrored doors was probably bought by Buchanan or Lincoln because the house had no closets; the shallow case beside it with a flowered curtain was fitted with exercise equipment. In this and many other pictures, Frances Benjamin Johnston—one of the first women to win fame as a news photographer—compiled a unique record of the White House in the 1890's. Here she caught not only the period's fondness for pattern upon pattern, but also the mansion's typical mixture of the stately and the purely personal: the grandeur of the antique bed, a homely crocheted pillowcase.

Expansion for an overcrowded house: With Mrs. Benjamin Harrison's encouragement, architect Fred D. Owen produced the first definite plans for enlarging the Executive Mansion. An immense new greenhouse extended across the south grounds in his most extravagant scheme (top). Cleveland's proposal of 1896 also included two large wings, but related them more successfully to the historic house. McKinley's 1900 model presents cupolas—an idea borrowed from the original wings of the Capitol.

the East Room, hair mattresses, marble mantels, curtains, matting, carpets, cuspidors, and an old globe of the world that once belonged to President Grant's daughter Nellie.

Along with assorted repairs to modernize the mansion, Arthur called in the famous Louis C. Tiffany of New York to redecorate the state rooms in a manner that foreshadowed Art Nouveau. He found little to do in the East Room but adorn the ceiling with silver and tones of ivory; his famous stained-glass screen (pages 130-31) in the Entrance Hall, now known only by black-and-white photographs, interlaced American eagles and flags "in the Arabian method."

None of Tiffany's major contributions were altered for Mrs. Cleveland in 1886. New lace curtains, fresh paint, touches of regilding, and diligent cleaning prepared the residence for the bride of the only President to marry in the mansion. In January 1887 she held her first reception and the first of her Saturday afternoon levees to let working women meet the Lady of the White House as women of society were free to do. (Only after 1900 did the term "First Lady" come into general use.)

Just how President Benjamin Harrison fitted his family into five bedrooms taxes imagination and record. It included his wife, her 90-year-old father, her sister and then a niece; son Russell, his wife, their daughter; daughter Mary McKee, two infants. Mrs. Harrison soon began a campaign for enlarging and improving the White House.

She ordered mold caused by faulty plumbing scrubbed off old walls, had layers of rotting floorboards peeled out of ground-floor rooms, and settled down to her hobby of painting china. She decorated cracker boxes, flowerpot saucers, and chocolate jugs—the greenhouses provided azaleas and orchids to copy. Her investigation of an old china closet led to the White House china collection, which represents almost every President through Lyndon B. Johnson and now contains pieces from the service added by Ronald Reagan.

Her interest in history inspired the idea of a "Historical Art Wing" for the enlarged mansion, but that project perished in the wake of a spat over patronage. The mansion was refurbished, with 30-inch-deep panels of blue glass decorated with gold scrollwork at the top of the Blue Room windows. Harrison found the new rooms "much improved," but wrote that the "greatest beauty of all" was in the bathroom "with the white tile and marble and porcelain-lined tub. They would tempt a duck to wash himself every day."

What Americans liked in the late 19th century, generally speaking, probably shows most vividly in the Harrisons' rooms (pages 134-35): the comfort of abundance in figured wallpaper, figured carpets, figured upholstery, tassels and fringe, furniture with curlicues cut by jigsaw, would-be Turkish cushions. An age enchanted by prosperity found the American furniture made about 1800 plain to the point of indecency.

Elaboration reached its zenith and by the McKinley Administration had begun to recede. Panels in the Blue Room evoked the simpler decor

In the grounds of the
White House, the cen-
tury between 1802 and
1902 brought impressive
change. Just when the
first greenhouse on the
east side appeared is
uncertain, but documen-
tary evidence places one
on the west grounds in
1857. By 1900 green-
houses (above) to supply
the mansion with cut
flowers and potted
plants had spread west
and south of the house.
The official in charge,
Col. Theodore A. Bing-
ham, fought in vain to
save a camellia house in
1902. For most of the
1800's the North Portico
provided the principal

door for guests; as early as President John Tyler's term, large crowds (left) departed by way of improvised bridges at windows—usually set up outside the East Room. Finally in 1902 a major renovation added an entrance at the east, swept away all the greenhouses, and erected the temporary West Wing of offices (above). The classic lines of the south façade contrast vividly with the ornament of a Victorian gatehouse probably from the 1870's —and with the plain little house for the guard dog (right).

of the Louis XVI style. With pale carpeting and walls, white counter-panes on thin-railed brass beds, and white upholstery, the McKinleys' northwest bedroom rivaled in lightness the somber state of Harrison's chamber. From the chandelier, a wire trailed down to the white-ruffled electric lamp on the table below. (The Harrisons were wary of the intricate, patched-together electrical system.) But Victoriana still reigned through most of the State Floor.

Like Cleveland's effort to get the mansion enlarged, McKinley's failed. As the centennial of the Capital drew near, a movement developed with the dream of restoring the city to meet the visions of George Washington and the plans drawn by Pierre Charles L'Enfant. Many agreed with architect Glenn Brown that the White House should also be enlarged and restored to this historic ideal.

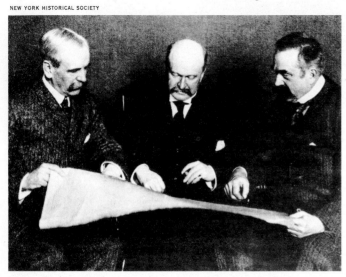

Architects of the 1902 renovation and expansion of the White House ordered by Theodore Roosevelt: from left, William R. Mead, Charles F. McKim, and Stanford White.

Thrust into the mansion by McKinley's assassination in 1901, Theodore Roosevelt dismissed suggestions that the President might live anywhere else, agreed that he should have offices outside the house, and called in the most prominent firm of architects in the country, McKim, Mead & White, known for their work in the historic style called "Colonial." With appropriation in hand as of June 1902, T. R. insisted on an October deadline for the new offices, with more leeway for the state rooms.

They found the Ground Floor in bad condition, and most of the State Floor settling dangerously. On the second story, flooring needed total replacement. Rainwater was still channeled through the walls in hollowed-out logs; the sanitary system defied description; obsolete wiring, its insulation worn off, had charred the wooden beams; lack of safe exits made the servants' rooms in the attic potential death-traps. Working at top speed, McKim, Mead & White reconstructed the interior throughout, excavating a new basement for the heating system.

They swept away the conservatories—"Smash the glass houses!" T. R. ordered—restored Jefferson's west pavilion to lead to the new Executive Offices, and rebuilt the east pavilion to shelter visitors arriving at a new east entrance. (By chance, Glenn Brown—who assisted in the renovation—learned from a New Jersey architect that an east pavilion had been pulled down in 1869 and by 1900 had been generally forgotten.) They provided cloakroom space, an exasperating need since the days when Jackson's admirers hung their coats on the fence outside.

Charles McKim's painstaking decoration of the State Floor obliterated the proud luxuries of the Victorians. The East Room emerged with the

East approaches, before and after: The east gate offered access to the
grounds—a shortcut for pedestrians—but no entrance to the mansion
suited for large gatherings until 1902. Then a portico that would hold 500
people and a porte cochere, capable of sheltering three carriages at once,
came into service; an arcade in the restored pavilion led to the mansion.

The enlarged and redecorated State Dining Room of 1902 (above) combined the classical taste of Charles McKim and the individual preferences
of Theodore Roosevelt. Wallpaper deeply bordered with floral motifs and
festoons gave way to fielded panels of burl oak. Trophy heads gazed
blankly over reproductions of Queen Anne chairs. Doubling the seating
capacity here put an end to scenes of make-do magnificence in the East
Room, adorned at right for a dinner honoring Prince Henry of Prussia
before alterations began. A stereopticon slide caught detail, from smilax
garlands to cut glass. The makers of this " 'artisque coleur' stereograph,"
describing the scene, asserted proudly: "It must have seemed to the
German prince very much like a dinner in a Christmas tree. . . ."

aspect it keeps today. Parquet floors gleamed uncarpeted—but T. R. put a polar-bear pelt in the Green Room. Along with Arthur's gaily tiled floor and Harrison's elaborate frescoes, the Tiffany screen passed into oblivion; the Entrance Hall took on the plain composure of stone. Spare, austere, consciously historic, the White House entered its second century.

Ever since 1902, an authentic look of the early years of the republic has been the ideal for those decorating the state rooms. Freewheeling incongruities vanished—such as adornments of the "Corridor" in 1898: delicate blue Venetian glass vases decorated with boars' heads, selected by Mrs. Grant; chairs made of elk antlers, from Arthur's term. When no antiques were available, reproductions served.

Although construction of the West Wing had finally ended the noisy inconveniences of a half-public second floor, the demands of a house for a nation left the private quarters none too large. Ellen Axson Wilson had attic space transformed into extra guest rooms and an artist's studio for herself; in 1927 Hoban's long-deferred third story took shape.

Hoping that the American people would help to furnish the White House, Grace Goodhue Coolidge helped persuade Congress to authorize the acceptance of appropriate antiques as gifts. A group appointed to evaluate such pieces continued to serve, under varying designations, through the Eisenhower years. Before leaving the mansion, Mrs. Coolidge had fitted out the Green Room— and had finished crocheting a spread for the Lincoln bed, consigned to storage by the Tafts, brought out for the Wilsons, and sent off again by the Hardings.

President Herbert Hoover recalled from storage four of Lincoln's Cabinet chairs, and grouped them with other furniture of the Lincoln-Grant era in his second-floor study—later his office after a fire in the West Wing in 1929. Mrs. Hoover catalogued White House furnishings and commissioned copies of furniture used by James Monroe.

To Franklin and Eleanor Roosevelt, wrote one of their guests, "a chair was something to sit down on . . . a table was something to put things on and a wall was something to be covered with . . . pictures of sentimental value." Their own rooms re-created rooms at Hyde Park (though the housekeeper said the rug in Mrs. Roosevelt's room was so historic you caught your heels in it); other upstairs bedrooms had furnishings that might have come from "an old and ultrarespectable summer resort hotel" or "a W.P.A. Arts and Crafts Project." The dingiest items were replaced in 1939, during a general sprucing-up to receive Their Britannic Majesties, George VI and Elizabeth, but the Roosevelts paid minimal attention to interior decorating in the midst of the Great Depression and World War II.

In 1934, rebuilding in the West Wing added underground working space; a new East Wing, hurriedly put up in World War II, supplied three stories of offices and the first White House bomb shelter.

War and cold war did not keep President Harry S. Truman from taking a lively interest in the architecture of the mansion, but his controversial balcony (page 148) was hardly finished when the building gave signs of collapsing. The investigation he ordered in February 1948 grew longer as its discoveries grew more alarming; the Trumans moved into Blair House — across Pennsylvania Avenue from the White House — while architects and engineers moved into action.

Between the 1902 steel of the first floor and the 1927 steel of the third, the carrying timbers of 1817 — riddled through the years by heating or ventilating flues, plumbing, and electrical conduits — were splitting under prolonged strain. "It is a wonderful thing," mused an engineer, "to contemplate the abuses that materials of construction sometimes will undergo before failure."

The architects of 1902 worked under time restrictions, those of 1927 under financial limitations. In 1949, at the President's request, Congress set up a Commission on Renovation of the Executive Mansion free of constraints. Members of the commission sensed a different necessity: to save the house as a symbol dear to Americans.

Various proposals called for demolishing the mansion completely and reproducing it with walls of granite or limestone or marble. But the old sandstone outer walls, with their broad footings and something like their original load, had survived in reasonable condition. Taking them down, as the commission felt and one member said, would be substantial and quite unnecessary desecration.

FRANCES BENJAMIN JOHNSTON, LIBRARY OF CONGRESS

Private stairway rises from the west end of the Cross Hall to the family quarters. The staircase was removed and the space added to the State Dining Room in 1902.

Out went furniture, chandeliers, mantelpieces from 1817 and 1902, paneling numbered and tagged for re-installation, and ornamental plasterwork — some of the sagging decorative plaster in the East Room weighed 70 pounds per square foot, but the workmen needed a jeweler's touch. Then partitions and floors were dismantled, steel shoring was installed, and the bulldozers began digging.

With concrete underpinning the old walls, a new two-story basement and new foundations, a new steel frame, the Executive Mansion returned to life, its interior restored with fidelity. Only the main stairway changed dramatically, descending now to the Entrance Hall for additional dignity. *(Continued on page 150)*

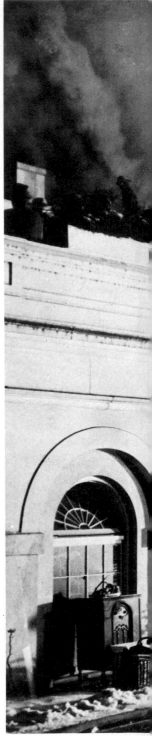

Raising the mansion's roof in 1927 for the construction of a new third story revealed some of the old wooden drainage system for rainwater. Crumbling ends of thick beams bore out an official warning to President Coolidge in 1923 that the roof had decayed to the point of danger. A chute at the South Portico carried down debris as crews working under tarpaulins removed second-floor ceilings, added steel girders, constructed and roofed a story of 18 rooms for storage, servants, and guests.

Fire in the West Wing on Christmas Eve, 1929, brought President Hoover from the dinner table to supervise the removal of papers from the Oval Office. Rescued items stand by a window; Mr. Hoover watches from the roof at left. During reconstruction he worked first in his "Lincoln Study" (the Lincoln Bedroom), then in the State-War-Navy Building (the Executive Office Building) next door. The Truman renovation included fireproofing, supplemented by a fire-detection system in 1965.

Jutting awnings broke the lines of the South Portico—if not the full heat of summer—before President Truman added a much-discussed balcony at the second-floor level in 1948. New wooden shades, which rolled up when not in use, did not reappear after the major renovation that soon proved necessary. Trembling chandeliers, cracking plaster, and floors which sagged and swayed prompted a months-long inspection; architects and engineers found the building dangerously weakened. The outer walls stood intact, braced by steel, while the Trumans lived at Blair House and workmen carefully dismantled the interior. After bulldozers had dug a new two-story basement, rebuilding began on new foundations with new load-bearing materials. By October 9, 1951, a crew was laying subflooring in the second-story corridor. After 27 months' work, with historic items painstakingly replaced, the Trumans moved back into the White House on March 27, 1952.

President Truman hoped to furnish the White House with items from its past and with fine antiques. His relations with Congress were often stormy; the budget proved inadequate. He did, however, receive some antiques as gifts. With television, Mr. Truman—and later Mrs. John F. Kennedy—guided fellow citizens through the White House room by room, and public interest in its decor increased perceptibly.

During Dwight D. Eisenhower's second term, the Biddle vermeil collection was bequeathed to the White House, and in 1960 the Diplomatic Reception Room was refurnished in the style of the Federal period.

Early in 1961, Mrs. Kennedy undertook to acquire appropriate items, forming the Fine Arts Committee for the White House. Museum experts and a curatorial staff assisted its work. A Special Committee on Paintings soon followed.

In the third-floor solarium, an enlarged version of Mrs. Coolidge's "sky parlor," a decorating team hangs new chintz draperies and sorts out a new set of casual bamboo furniture on February 14, 1952.

In September, the 87th Congress passed legislation providing that furniture of "historic or artistic interest" might become "inalienable" property of the mansion, with provision for the Smithsonian Institution to hold on loan any object not on display or in use. In the Ground Floor Corridor and the "principal public rooms" of the first floor, it recognized a "museum character" worthy of "primary attention."

By Executive Order, on March 7, 1964, President Lyndon B. Johnson established the Committee for the Preservation of the White House. Its duties include making "recommendations as to the articles of furniture . . . . which shall be used or displayed in the public rooms . . . and as to the decor and arrangements best suited to enhance the historic and artistic values of the White House." This order also provided for a permanent curator.

During President Richard M. Nixon's years in office, the White House acquired for its collection numerous valuable pieces of furniture and American paintings, among them portraits from life of several Presidents and First Ladies. Mrs. Nixon began a major program of much-needed renovation in 1969. During the next five years all of the principal rooms on the State Floor and Ground Floor were redecorated. President and Mrs. Gerald R. Ford continued to support efforts toward the preservation of the historic character of the Presidential Mansion.

Red damask—pierced for sconces—shimmers on parlor walls, fragile caryatids of Carrara marble stand unscarred, and on March 20 skilled hands lift a portrait of Wilson as the Red Room assumes its elegance again.

Designed as a warm and livable sitting area, the third-floor center hall received a total refurbishing in 1981. Renovations begun in the Coolidge Administration had transformed a shallow attic into private living quarters.

President Jimmy Carter and his family showed particular interest in furnishings associated with former White House inhabitants. Mrs. Carter also added 34 American paintings to the permanent collection.

Interest in the White House stimulated by Mrs. Ronald Reagan made possible a major redecoration of second- and third-floor rooms, as well as special preservation projects for rooms on the State Floor. Many fine pieces of early 19th-century American furniture already in the collection were retrieved from storage, refurbished, and returned to service in the mansion. Among new acquisitions accepted by the Reagans for the White House was Albert Bierstadt's "View of the Rocky Mountains," which hangs in the Red Room.

Donors all over the country who have given articles of museum quality to the White House can assume with confidence that the care of their gifts has become a public trust. Today the curator's office not only oversees the preservation of White House treasures but also, since 1978, has maintained a computer inventory that includes their origin, acquisition, associations with historical figures, location, and condition.

Future generations can expect data more exact than the associations that clustered around Jackson's Mexican chair or the memoirs that happened to mention such furnishings. A list compiled in April 1898, with the help of usher Thomas F. Pendel, illustrates the uncertainties of tradition and the pathos of memory: for the State Dining Room, "Brass pheasant with chicks—Mrs. Grant. . . . Five fruit stands—perhaps Thomas Jefferson. Set of chairs—straight pieces in back—New York City—Arthur. Side board & side table before Lincoln. Plateau—T.J.(?). White marble mantels—there since house was built." The plateau in fact dated from 1817, the mantels from 1818.

For generations Americans considering the White House judged it with reference to two distinct norms: a great palace of Europe (whether seen or imagined) and the home of a gentleman (a standard that altered rapidly indeed). These criteria diverged so widely that defining an ideal Executive Mansion was not easy—though of course every citizen and visitor freely passed judgment.

In 1834 a thoughtful, anonymous writer spoke gravely to the point: "This is the only PALACE in the United States. The chief magistrate of the United States has justly a spacious house, while in office, at the charge of the nation, and for the honor of the nation; and yet we cannot but hope, that as little of European parade and display, and especially of luxury or extravagance, will be found there in future, as in years past since our republic was founded."

Now the White House ranks as a norm in its own right. Comparisons still come naturally, though less obviously: The number of rooms in the private family section—nine—approximates the number in a suburban home. But the ritual of state occasions speaks not for individual but for national dignity. Suited to its time, as George Washington hoped, in established maturity the White House looks "beyond the present day."

THE
PRESIDENTS

George Washington	*April 30, 1789-March 3, 1797*
John Adams	*March 4, 1797-March 3, 1801*
Thomas Jefferson	*March 4, 1801-March 3, 1809*
James Madison	*March 4, 1809-March 3, 1817*
James Monroe	*March 4, 1817-March 3, 1825*
John Quincy Adams	*March 4, 1825-March 3, 1829*
Andrew Jackson	*March 4, 1829-March 3, 1837*
Martiñ Van Buren	*March 4, 1837-March 3, 1841*
William Henry Harrison	*March 4, 1841-April 4, 1841*
John Tyler	*April 6, 1841-March 3, 1845*
James K. Polk	*March 4, 1845-March 3, 1849*
Zachary Taylor	*March 5, 1849-July 9, 1850*
Millard Fillmore	*July 10, 1850-March 3, 1853*
Franklin Pierce	*March 4, 1853-March 3, 1857*
James Buchanan	*March 4, 1857-March 3, 1861*
Abraham Lincoln	*March 4, 1861-April 15, 1865*
Andrew Johnson	*April 15, 1865-March 3, 1869*
Ulysses S. Grant	*March 4, 1869-March 3, 1877*
Rutherford B. Hayes	*March 3, 1877-March 3, 1881*
James A. Garfield	*March 4. 1881-September 19, 1881*
Chester A. Arthur	*September 20, 1881-March 3, 1885*
Grover Cleveland	*March 4, 1885-March 3, 1889*
Benjamin Harrison	*March 4, 1889-March 3, 1893*
Grover Cleveland	*March 4, 1893-March 3, 1897*
William McKinley	*March 4, 1897-September 14, 1901*
Theodore Roosevelt	*September 14, 1901-March 3, 1909*
William H. Taft	*March 4, 1909-March 3, 1913*
Woodrow Wilson	*March 4, 1913-March 3, 1921*
Warren G. Harding	*March 4, 1921-August 2, 1923*

Calvin Coolidge	*August 3, 1923-March 3, 1929*
Herbert Hoover	*March 4, 1929-March 3, 1933*
Franklin D. Roosevelt	*March 4, 1933-April 12, 1945*
Harry S. Truman	*April 12, 1945-January 20, 1953*
Dwight D. Eisenhower	*January 20, 1953-January 20, 1961*
John F. Kennedy	*January 20, 1961-November 22, 1963*
Lyndon B. Johnson	*November 22, 1963-January 20, 1969*
Richard M. Nixon	*January 20, 1969-August 9, 1974*
Gerald R. Ford	*August 9, 1974-January 20, 1977*
Jimmy Carter	*January 20, 1977-January 20, 1981*
Ronald Reagan	*January 20, 1981-*

INDEX

Boldface indicates illustrations.

Additional References

The reader may wish to consult books on or by individual Presidents and their families for information on the White House during specific administrations, as well as the following books and articles for material related to the White House:

Books: Lonnelle Aikman, *The Living White House;* Wilhelmus Bogart Bryan, *A History of the National Capital* (2 volumes); Commission on the Renovation of the Executive Mansion, *Report . . . , 1952;* Alonzo Fields, *My 21 Years in the White House;* Bess Furman, *White House Profile;* Constance McLaughlin Green, *Washington: Village and Capital, 1800-1878* and *Washington: Capital City, 1879-1950;* Irwin Hood (Ike) Hoover, *Forty-two Years in the White House;* Amy La Follette Jensen, *The White House and its Thirty-five Families;* Margaret Brown Klapthor, *Official White House China: 1789 to the Present* and *The First Ladies;* Henrietta Nesbitt, *White House Diary;* William Ryan and Desmond Guinness, *The White House: An Architectural History;* William Seale, *The President's House* (2 volumes); Esther Singleton, *The Story of the White House* (2 volumes); Margaret Baynard Smith, *The First Forty Years of Washington Society;* U. S. Committee for the Preservation of the White House, *Report . . . , 1964-1969;* U. S. Senate Document Number 197, 57th Congress, 2nd Session, "Restoration of the White House. Message of the President of the United States Transmitting the Report of the Architects"; J. B. West, *Upstairs at the White House.*

Periodical: *White House History,* Volume One, 1983.

Articles: Lonnelle Aikman, "The Living White House," NATIONAL GEOGRAPHIC, November 1966; Clement E. Conger, "Decorative Arts at the White House," *Antiques,* July 1979; Hans Huth, "The White House Furniture at the Time of Monroe," *Gazette des Beaux Arts,* January 1946; Marie G. Kimball, "The Original Furnishings of the White House," *Antiques,* June and July 1929; Margaret Brown Klapthor, "A First Lady and a New Frontier, 1800," *Historic Preservation,* volume 15, number 3, 1963, and "Benjamin Latrobe and Dolley Madison Decorate the White House, 1809-1811," *Contributions from the Museum of History and Technology: Paper 49;* "President and Mrs. Ronald Reagan at the White House," *Architectural Digest,* December 1981; Marvin Sadik, "Paintings from the White House," *The Connoisseur,* July 1976; Berry B. Tracy, "Federal Period Furniture," *The Connoisseur,* July 1976; John Wilmerding, "The American painting collection of the White House," *Antiques,* July 1979.

Composition for *The White House: An Historic Guide* by the Typographic section of National Geographic Production Services, Pre-Press Division. Printed and bound by R. R. Donnelley & Sons Co., Willard, OH. Color separations by the Lanman Progressive Company, Washington, D.C.

The President's Park—This drawing is based on an aerial photograph and a plan drawn by the National Park Service. The trees and other landscape features shown in darker green are associated with Presidents and are identified in the key at right.

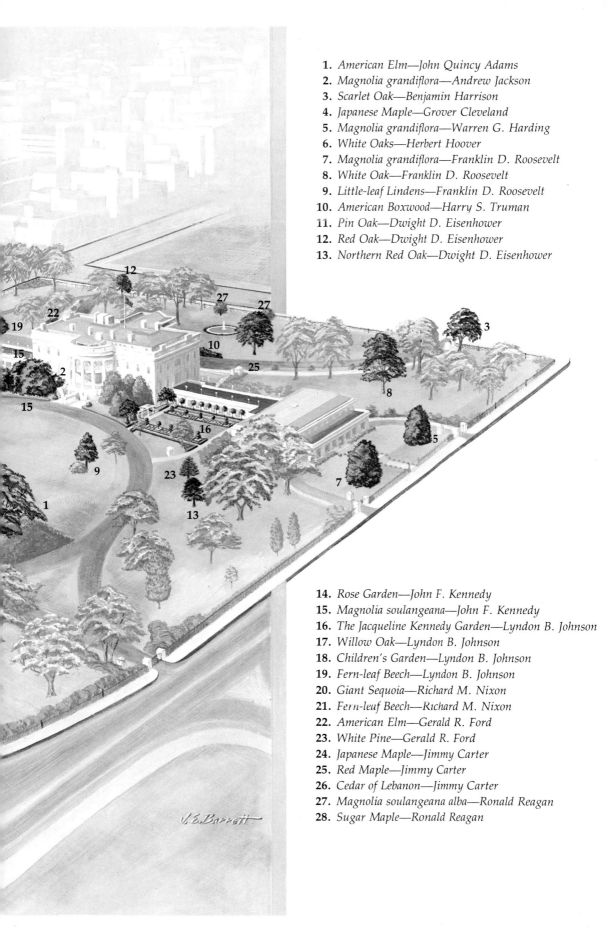

1. *American Elm—John Quincy Adams*
2. *Magnolia grandiflora—Andrew Jackson*
3. *Scarlet Oak—Benjamin Harrison*
4. *Japanese Maple—Grover Cleveland*
5. *Magnolia grandiflora—Warren G. Harding*
6. *White Oaks—Herbert Hoover*
7. *Magnolia grandiflora—Franklin D. Roosevelt*
8. *White Oak—Franklin D. Roosevelt*
9. *Little-leaf Lindens—Franklin D. Roosevelt*
10. *American Boxwood—Harry S. Truman*
11. *Pin Oak—Dwight D. Eisenhower*
12. *Red Oak—Dwight D. Eisenhower*
13. *Northern Red Oak—Dwight D. Eisenhower*

14. *Rose Garden—John F. Kennedy*
15. *Magnolia soulangeana—John F. Kennedy*
16. *The Jacqueline Kennedy Garden—Lyndon B. Johnson*
17. *Willow Oak—Lyndon B. Johnson*
18. *Children's Garden—Lyndon B. Johnson*
19. *Fern-leaf Beech—Lyndon B. Johnson*
20. *Giant Sequoia—Richard M. Nixon*
21. *Fern-leaf Beech—Richard M. Nixon*
22. *American Elm—Gerald R. Ford*
23. *White Pine—Gerald R. Ford*
24. *Japanese Maple—Jimmy Carter*
25. *Red Maple—Jimmy Carter*
26. *Cedar of Lebanon—Jimmy Carter*
27. *Magnolia soulangeana alba—Ronald Reagan*
28. *Sugar Maple—Ronald Reagan*